Awakening

With

OddJobBob

Awakening

With

OddJobBob

The True Story of a Handyman and his unexpected journey of Enlightenment

For privacy reasons, some names, locations, and dates may have been changed.

Book Cover by Author

Edition Number 1 edition 2023

For Lesley

The Love of My Life and Best Friend

Lucky, Blessed, Protected

My Thanks and Love go to my Children their partners and Grand Children, who are always a joy to be with.

Also, my wider family and beyond, who've taught me so much.

Thank you to Jo, Lucy, Nat, and Sharon for your feedback on my earliest drafts.

I deeply appreciate all the interactions I've had with others over my Life, although it's highly unlikely I always did at the time! So, for what it's worth, thank you to everyone I've ever met.

Contents

Preface

"To be, or not to be, that is the question."

Fear is the emotion that blocks our ability to see. I should know because I also know that I have lived in fear for most of my life. I didn't know it at the time, because like everything else that made me feel uncomfortable or inadequate, I buried it deep inside.

My fears were so deep I didn't realise they were even there.

I believed I was a perfectly normal, balanced but imperfect Human, trying to be the best and happiest he could be.

Like most of my beliefs, I discovered I was wrong.

I never imagined I would write a book – ever and didn't plan to write this.

This started as an essay in early 2023. After a while I decided it needed chapters and this is the result.

I've used the term Awakening as opposed to Awake, because Awake suggests you're no longer Asleep and that feels arrogant to me. To be Awake means that you pierce through **all** the veils of reality and if there's one thing I now **know**, there's **more** than one.

This is my attempt to put into coherent order my process of Awakening so far and my new understanding of who we are, why the World is at is, and our purpose here.

It's my book of tiny ledges of knowing.

My First **knowing** is that our Prime Human instinct is Survival, which is shared by all living organisms. This is necessary, particularly here on Earth because we exist in a predatory system.

It is hard wired into our every waking moment that we must breathe, drink, eat and have shelter. It's so fundamental that, for the most part, we aren't consciously aware of it.

Fear is an integral part of our survival instinct.

My earliest recollection of conquering fear was when I learned to swim. I'm sure you reading this have similar memories. Something you found perhaps terrifying but where you found the will to master the challenge.

I've concluded that if there was any one thing responsible for my blindness to the veils of reality it was Fear. For whatever reason(s) I didn't have the will to pull back the veil earlier in my life.

Paradoxically when I did find the will to do so, it was anger that broke the spell, along with becoming reconciled with the inevitability of my own Death. I simply reached a point where I was no longer afraid of it.

For someone who believes themselves to be solely a Human body, this book will be the ravings of the insane. For someone who believes they are more than just their physical body, hopefully the opposite will apply.

From my own anecdotal experience, I have met and talked to many other people who share my apparent psychosis of Awakening. We have all arrived at the same point of view entirely independently of each other.

Some are further along the path than others, but I can see the World the same way as some others, which is a magical experience. By magical I mean it's beyond apparent explanation as the World we see is **not** the same World as the majority do.

I suppose it's like a muggle suddenly being able to see the Magical World of Harry Potter. (Sort of Lol)

I try to keep this Knowing to the front and centre of my mind. The journey I've been on has taken me to the edge of reason. I had no choice anyway, there's something within that compels me.

Many Awakening people describe feeling a sense of urgency when they first begin Awakening. They have a Mission and a Purpose here but don't know what it is or how to complete it.

It would appear that writing this is part of my particular Mission. It's unlikely to be a best seller, but that isn't important. What is important is that it helps those who are Awakening and who can use the information it contains.

I've found the Universe has the knack of making things happen.

Like Magic.

Introduction

"The web of our life is of a mingled yarn, good and ill together".

I don't know about you, but I change a bit every day. I wake each morning knowing who I am, and all my memories are as before, but when I look back over time I can see and know I'm **different** besides being older. It hasn't always been like this.

My family have always considered me a bit odd. Prone to daydreaming with a strange imagination. Nevertheless, I unconsciously adopted various archetypes as a I progressed from childhood into adulthood and my life unfolded in an unremarkable way.

I don't want to diminish the importance or value of those 56 years. I experienced everything I could have wished for both good and bad, but I wasn't consciously aware of who or what I was.

I'm not sure I'm aware of who I really am now, but I do know that I'm **more** than my physical body. How much more and **what** that more is has become my ongoing mission, when I'm not putting up shelves etc.

In the past I didn't feel I was **pretending** to be something I wasn't, but I was. I embodied the character I was projecting as authentically as anyone. My emotional reactions of love, lust, anger, envy, joy, happiness etc. were (as far as I was concerned) real and still are.

At some point I came to believe that those memories, behaviours, and characteristics were who I was. Don't we all?

My adult archetypes: I have been a Son, a Father, a Husband, a Heterosexual, a Delivery Driver, a Banker, a Parachutist, a Salesman, a Director, and a Handyman. **We can all write similar lists**. **None** of them describe who we really are, which is a bit of a paradox, but not the only one by a long way.

I would have described myself **then** as open-minded, responsible, caring, opinionated, intelligent, adaptable, sceptical, agnostic, informed, serious, happy, loving, resigned and content. I was looking forward to retiring, or at least something less physically demanding.

I was lucky to be in a position where I could retire at any time, but as I had no idea how long I was going to live I was just plodding on. 2019 had been a good year for us. Our business had been trading for ten years and this year had been the best so far financially, but it had also been the most exhausting.

The more work we did, the more we earned, but the result was that I spent most weekends trying to do as little as possible while my aching muscles and joints could have some rest!

Our three children had all grown into fine adults. Two were living independently. Our eldest was happily engaged, our second eldest was married with two children, while our youngest and her fiancé were staying with us before a working holiday in Canada.

In early January 2020, my daughter asked me what I knew about the virus outbreak in China. I'd recently speed read something on the web and concluded it was like the other SARS or MERS outbreaks so told her not to worry, it would be like the other outbreaks – a nothing burger.

The following evening, I thought back to how dismissive I'd been and decided I'd look at it in a bit more detail. I went from dismissive to full blown **shit!** I studied every article I could find and was astonished, as events unfolded, that almost no-one else around me saw what was coming until well into March.

I was hungry for knowledge. I wanted to understand more. I found plenty of information thanks to the WHO, Gates Foundation and academia and it became increasingly clear that this was the big one – Disease X – probably a Coronavirus, for which there would be no vaccine and no obvious cure.

Events unfolded. Citizens keeling over in Wuhan, overflowing beds in Italy and the first few cases in the UK. Other reports such as air travellers being infected in their seats and a cruise liner full of pensioners were finding their way into the mainstream. It was coming.

I found an interesting thread on Reddit, where a group of Junior doctors were comparing notes. The upshot was being male, elderly, or obese were all significant factors and the best proactive defence was to take Vit D and Zinc.

In the middle of March, I found myself buying bottles of Vitamins, some for us, and some for my 90-year-old Mum. I'd already stocked up on toilet rolls in February! The last items I bought were some bags of sand and cement.

March 23rd, 2020, and we were in Lockdown.

What a fucked-up experience that was! I visited my local shop more than once (for cigarettes) in the first week alone and scolded myself in the journal I'd just begun keeping. I then concentrated on re-laying the patio, which kept me busy for a week or so.

Then the weather turned nice. Really nice. Clear Blue skies, light breezes. Spring was suddenly exploding all around, but rather than stop and observe it, I got lost in trying to help solve the pandemic.

I would sit in the garden looking for hope on my smartphone and getting tanned. What about a breath test for Covid? There are people working on the tech – how could I help? The short answer was nothing.

Up until lockdown the business was ahead of 2019. Now with no income coming in the best we could do was furlough ourselves. It helped, but with all the other costs still there, it began dying a slow death.

At least the English Chief Medical Officer was a virology specialist. I hoped that the right decisions were being taken by the right people at the right time. Masks were essential. Lockdowns were the only protection, until a vaccine could be developed.

By the middle of April, I was anxious to do **something** besides sit around, so made the decision that from the beginning of May, we'd do outdoor jobs. I came off furlough and went back out into the World.

It was weird. Much less traffic on the roads and the few pedestrians about were mostly desperate to avoid coming close to each other. Other than that, it was perfectly normal. The weather and the wildlife were oblivious.

I was an obedient and concerned citizen, even volunteering for the vaccine trials. I wasn't called up, and I was very critical of any rule breakers when it came to the restrictions as it was all for the greater good etc.

I knew that our response to the pandemic was poor. It had all the hall marks of incompetence, but what could I do? I was losing faith in the system, but I didn't have the courage to admit it, particularly to myself.

I would hear myself thinking that it was Science that got us into this mess & Science would get us out. The Lab leak was (in my view at the time) the most likely cause of the nightmare.

A sense that something wasn't quite right was growing within me. I didn't know what it was, but the feeling wouldn't go away.

I spent my days doing jobs and my evenings glued to the latest News. The year unfolded and then something quite unexpected happened. My doubts about the authorities gradually became more intense until on 1.1.21 **my belief system completely collapsed**.

I asked myself **why** the authorities consistently got things wrong. I was **angry.** Not so much at **them** but **me. Why** was I so wilfully naïve? **Why** did I believe everything was just incompetence?

And then, as if a switch had been flicked in my mind, I **Knew.**

It **wasn't** just incompetence and **yes,** my naivety was wilful. My **belief** system, the same as just about everyone else's, had **conditioned me** into either **accepting or ignoring** whatever lies were being told as the alternative was **too disturbing**, **frightening, or unsettling** to even consider.

This sense of **Knowing** is difficult to describe as I've only experienced it before a few times in my Life where I'd come to a knowing which **reversed** a **belief** e.g. Santa Claus isn't real and afterward that **knowing** is unshakeable.

I wasn't frightened, but I **was** horrified. Oh my God, I **must** be wrong. This was just too sick to accept, but I had no choice. It was what it was. I was learning a new truth. **All** the Authorities we defer to and rely on are systemically corrupt.

Once the scales have fallen from your eyes, you can't put them back. My moment of revelation had occurred in the early hours of 1.1.21, which was quite a personal and abstract coincidence.

As an 18-year-old I'd moved out of my childhood home to live with my elder sister and her new-born daughter. Our address was number 1121.

I no longer believed the News and found that I also didn't believe in accepted History, Science, or anything else for that matter. Almost everything I had formerly believed in was a lie.

Everything else was unchanged. Going to work for people, shopping, time with family, the weather, eating etc. were just the same as before. I simply **no longer** believed in the system and the impact of doing so was dramatic.

I didn't know it then, but I was **Awakening.** If you're reading this in the hope of becoming Awakened **that is not its purpose.** My hypothesis is that Awakening occurs spontaneously, so I don't expect these words to trigger anything, but it should be helpful as and when it does and **particularly if it already has**.

You may **think** you're Awakening, or **believe** you already are, but the perception shift I experienced was to that of **knowing**, which is different. As and when it happens you will just **know** that you've broken the spell.

I tried alerting my family, siblings, and children that the authorities and media were lying to us. They thought I was psychotic, so I stopped. To be perfectly honest I don't blame them. Had I been approached by anyone describing the World the way I now saw it; I'd have thought they were psychotic as well.

I was no longer seeing the World the way I wanted it to be. It had changed before my eyes. Everything on the TV news and most of what was online were bare-faced lies – how could they not see it?

I was seeing **through** the veil and seeing it how it actually was, or was I? I needed to know. I needed to **understand.** As my Awakening continued, so did the shocks. I reflected on what I understood of History and Politics and realised with **knowing** that they were a deceit, and this extended **as far back as I could see**.

It was like waking from a Dream, one which has been so real and convincing that it takes a while to realise you've been dreaming. When you realise the 'dream' has lasted 56 years it takes a lot of processing!

I'd been a Non-Playable Character (NPC) all my life! NPC's are the non-playable characters in video games. They might have dialogue, or they could just be random characters in the background. They are controlled by the Game, as opposed to by an individual player.

That seemed to be a pretty good metaphor for my existence to date, but as I discovered, it could just as accurately be applied to me now. I'm still the same as everybody else in most respects.

I couldn't watch the News or most of what was on TV; it made me nauseous. I couldn't listen to the Radio either, except classical music, which I'd not done in the past. It was curious. What was happening to me?

There was a Mountain of conspiracy theories to explore, and sure enough when I explored the alternate explanations to the accepted narrative, I discovered that amongst the tin foil hatters was more **truth** than I expected.

There was / is a problem though – misinformation and disinformation. The conspiracy World is full of it (by design) and this is a significant hurdle to overcome. I needed to apply my discernment and be unemotional and logical with what I found, which wasn't easy.

I sought and found others (online) who could see through the veil but found myself reluctant to commit to an alternative set of beliefs. My first set of beliefs had collapsed like a house of cards, and I didn't want to make the same mistake twice.

The media portrayal of Trump (and to an extent Brexit) had played a large part in my Awakening. I wasn't particularly passionate about or in favour of either, but I nursed a deeply held belief in Democracy and that results **must** be respected.

That belief was unceremoniously trampled on by the Mainstream media and politicians on the losing sides. Brexiteers and Trump supporters were ignorant, racist, misogynistic types who lacked any conception of the greater good.

To deride such people was portrayed as courageous and understandable, while anyone questioning this narrative was characterised at best as weak minded, and at worst as bigoted.

I found myself astonished that no-one else could see what I was seeing – it was just so obvious (I thought). As the years have passed, astonishment has transmuted into acceptance. Prior to Awakening I was the same as the majority - **blind**.

I think my blindness was ignorance. I'd never felt the need to do my own research. If the BBC reported something as a fact, it was a fact. It wasn't as if I was a citizen of some authoritarian regime. There was no need for me to check anything.

On reflection, this was a fear driven attitude. I didn't **want** to know about **anything** that contradicted my belief system.

When something did arise e.g. the invasion of Iraq, I did what was necessary to maintain my belief. When the troops went in and the weapons inspectors found no WMD's, the consensus view was that it didn't matter. Hussein was a bad guy, and the end justified the means.

Deep down I knew what had transpired was criminal, but no-one else I knew was making a fuss, I'd just ignore it as well. It's a form of mass hypnosis and very clever.

My life of ignoring uncomfortable things was over. Some part of me had died.

Shall we Play A Game?

I heard the 'going outside the box' expression for years before learning what it originally referred to and it's a puzzle - a literal puzzle, and it's a hard one. At least I found it was. Perhaps it'll be easier for you. Here it is:

Your challenge is to join all 9 dots using just 4 straight lines. The lines must go through the middle of all the dots without taking your pencil off the paper. Each line starts where the last one finishes.

Find a piece (or several pieces) of paper and a pencil and see if you can work it out. This is solvable, but really difficult for most, me included. A solution is at the back of this book. You can go straight to it or just look it up on the web.

If you do this **without** solving it, you will not experience the **'Aha'** moment of learning, and the likelihood is that you will not fully comprehend the deepest meaning of the puzzle.

Arguably this puzzle, and others like it, are gateways to greater levels of understanding and comprehension. Once something has become part of your consciousness you cannot unlearn it and it illustrates how something can be veiled – hidden in plain sight.

My journey of piercing through the veils of reality has kept to this infuriating trend. I haven't found anything that wasn't **already** there. Once you **see** it, it becomes obvious, but only **you** can do this. All I can do is describe what I see.

No-one can see it for you, or even force you to see. **Only you**.

The Handyman Approach

"A Fool thinks himself to be wise, but a wise man knows himself to be a fool"

I never thought about being a Handyman until about 9 months before I became one. It's not the sort of occupation that people aspire to. My archetypal image of a Handyman was a shabby old man with a beard who would drive around in a beaten-up Estate car full of junk.

Prior to becoming one, I'd worn a suit most of my working Life and I'd been successful. My last job had been as the head of a sales operation with seven sites and about 100 staff.

It ended in 2008 largely due to the financial crash. I was made redundant. It had happened twice before in my career. On the first occasion I'd almost broken down with the feelings of failure and the desperation to get a new job.

The second time wasn't as traumatic, but it was still awful. This time I was determined it was going to be the last time. The only way I could guarantee this was to start and run my own business, but doing what?

After reading an article that suggested turning a past time into an occupation, I realised that my main 'hobby' was DIY and so becoming a Handyman was a possible route to a new business.

I was still reasonably young (44) and fit but decided that **my** archetype would wear a uniform and drive around in a proper Van. After that my strategy was simple. I would focus on doing the basic things very well.

I'd keep my promises, be honest with customers, and treat them like I would like to be treated myself. Hopefully, I'd be able to earn a decent living and after a few years perhaps franchise it. On 1.1.09 we began trading as OddJobBob.

The first three years were pretty hard, but I was learning as I went along and by the fourth, I knew what I was doing, and could start to enjoy it more. In the fifth year I paid a consultant to look at franchising.

It cost me £5k to get a report that said the chances of successfully franchising the business were marginal as were the potential rewards. It would cost another £25k to find out if it would fly.

We decided not to find out. I let my ambition to be a successful entrepreneur go. In truth I enjoyed being a Handyman more than I enjoyed wearing a suit. I was earning a decent living anyway, so I'd just carry on.

Like many people, I'd carried an ambition to be a somebody, most of my working life. I suppose I was in a relatively small way during my time, but when I was a somebody, it felt uncomfortable a lot of the time.

I suppose it was because I knew deep down, I was acting. As a Handyman I could be more authentically me. I could also be a nobody. Having tasted the flavour of being a somebody, I didn't have the appetite for it anymore.

I could have trained to be a plumber, carpenter, electrician, or some other trade, but I enjoyed the variety of doing lots of different things. I also enjoy solving puzzles and being a Handyman brings lots of puzzles to solve.

Modern housing is unlike the housing of years ago. Sure, it **looks** the same, but it isn't. They need Electricity **and** Gas **and** running water – hot and cold. They are more like static machines than simple boxes with a doors and windows.

I suppose it's because someone decided it looks better that way, that most of what makes modern house's work is **concealed**.

I've lost count of the number of customers with broken toilets who complain that they can't even get the lid off the cistern, or they can't get a door to shut properly and don't understand why.

Every job is a puzzle. The customer describes an effect and I need to find the cause. Often, the cause is hidden and finding it is the key to resolving the problem.

Invariably, diagnosing the cause involves removing whatever is concealing it. It might just be a simple cover, but sometimes you must go through multiple layers and / or approach the issue from different angles.

I'd like to say every puzzle is fun, but when you're on your back in a bathroom with your head wedged between a dirty toilet and a slightly less dirty pedestal, it really isn't but someone has to do it.

In the past, people were more multi skilled, so it's interesting how few are today. We have been encouraged to become specialists in our career choices. We are steered to focus our efforts on a career and 'get someone in' to do the jobs at home.

Tenants often don't have a choice – the landlord sends someone in!

I did a job lagging a loft for a young couple who were tenants. He worked as a Nurse. She was a home Mum to two young kids. It was February 2021 and freezing cold. Halfway through I took a short break and had a chat with them. They were Awakening.

Or at least held the same view about the Authorities and Media. I've not seen or spoken to them since but was grateful for meeting them. I felt a bit less insane and was encouraged by the experience.

Awakening was an effect, so my Handyman brain turned its attention to the cause. To start with I needed to clarify exactly what the effect was:

1. I'd become conscious that I'd been formerly hypnotised.
2. Almost everyone I knew was hypnotised.
3. The foundations on which my ego had been built were no longer there.
4. I accepted that I'd been living a fantasy life and had been blind to reality.
5. I needed to understand.

For those who start Awakening this list is typical. Number 5 is called **Inquiry**. With no foundations, you go looking for new ones and there's no shortage of alternatives.

I'd looked at the Q posts and they were fascinating. The premise is simple - Q is an agent / are agents of the Deep State gone rogue. Its purpose is to catalyse a 'Great Awakening' of Humanity and replace the established control system.

At least that's how I've interpreted it. The posts revealed there really is a global network of criminal actors that are covertly running the World. Many are well known public figures, but many are not.

I didn't just take Q's word for it, I did my own research, and yes indeed the World is not only run by criminals, but it also appears it has been this way for a very long time, centuries at a minimum, but most likely longer.

This is **impossible** to accept if you're Asleep. We are conditioned to dismiss such notions as the stuff of conspiracy theory or dangerous, but it's possible to entertain theories without necessarily completely believing everything about them.

Awakening had already taught me that most of my existing Beliefs had been false. My conditioned need for **certainty** had been, in some part, responsible for my belief in the System. I realised I wasn't going to **believe** in anything anymore unless I **knew** it be a fact.

Q posts are clever and revealing to an open mind, but accepting everything they state as true, I don't think is wise. The same applies to all areas of Inquiry. I went in other directions: (**Please do your own research** – don't just take my word for **anything** that follows).

Chemtrails became noticeable to me. I'd seen them before but had not paid any attention to them. Now I was paying more attention to things and there were these strange trails appearing from time to time in the sky, so I researched it.

The biggest shock was discovering that they'd been first 'noticed' sometime in the 1970's. I've found photos I took pre-Awakening with loads of trails visible. I honestly hadn't noticed them at the time.

There is a LOT of stuff on Chemtrails. So much that it's impossible to settle on a complete theory, however one aspect can be deduced. The resources required to do it are considerable and it's a world-wide phenomenon.

Historical revisions were something else I looked at, such as Tartaria.

There are a lot of maps from antiquity that show a massive Empire called Tartaria or Tartary. You can find them online easily enough. It stretched from Eastern Europe to the Eastern Pacific coast. It seems to have disappeared from official History around the middle of the 18th Century.

My research led me to conclude that so little is now known of where, when and what Tartaria was, it's not possible to settle on a credible theory, however one aspect can be deduced.

The resources required to create this level of disinformation are considerable and it's a world-wide phenomenon.

The Pandemic was something that I now inquired about in an open-minded way as possible. It was challenging as there was so much to process. It is a mind field (not a misspelling).

I learned about Terrain theory and Germ theory. I Studied alternate theories where diseases are in fact due to environmental poisoning or parasitic infections, and all seem possible.

Then there was the Lab leak theory (any evidence appears to have been destroyed) and finally the deliberate release theory. So, take your pick.

I noticed something really odd though. The disappearance of Influenza.

In 2020 and 2021 the incidence of Influenza world-wide **evaporated**. According to the US Centre for Disease Control in the 2018 – 19 Flu season they estimated that at least 13 **million** US citizens developed Influenza. In the 2020 – 21 Flu season it was just 1,675 positive tests from about 890,000 patients.

https://www.cdc.gov/flu/season/faq-flu-season-2020-2021.htm

The word Influenza comes from Italian. It means **visitation** or **influence.** Millions of cases in both hemispheres have been recorded **every year** since 1918. Every year **except** 2020/21.

I don't claim to know the specific details of what has been going on. I don't need to know the minute details of a fraud to recognise one. There is no logical explanation for this, and the resources required to create this level of disinformation are considerable. Clearly, it's world-wide.

Mark Twain was quoted as saying 'It's easier to fool a man than convince him he's been fooled' and **I had been fooled**. All these contradictions I was finding, all in plain sight, how had I missed them? What was I still not seeing **now**?

I was getting closer to seeing the World as it was, but it wasn't really helping to progress my Awakening. I needed to find something deeper and more meaningful.

What was it all about? Why all the deception? Why am I waking up to this only now? Why not before? Do I know who I am? Why is this happening?

My inquiries revealed that people have been Awakening for centuries. It's generally referred to as becoming enlightened. Quite a few have been incarcerated in asylums over the years as a result.

Wilhelm Reich, an assistant to Sigmund Freud, who wrote about his experiences of visiting lunatic asylums in the early 20th century, concluded that most of the patients he saw were totally sane, but weren't acceptable within the insane society that prevailed at the time.

Awakening had collapsed my agnostic foundation. I no longer denied the existence of a creator. Its existence was now obvious to me, even if it appeared to be sadistic one. It was an unorthodox route to that conclusion but there it was.

It wasn't something that filled me with joy. There was a cruelty to what I was saw that suggested that God might not be anything like I'd been told by any religion.

I'd been exposed to quite a few religions during my life and none of them had made rational sense. As a child I didn't question it, but by my 40's I thought it was bizarre that effigies of Christ being **tortured on a cross** were revered. Had he been **beheaded** would people worship his head on a spear?

No religion acknowledged the Invisible control structure I could now perceive. There was only one rational explanation for this – they were all part of it or at least in on it.

There was / is certainly something magical or paranormal about Awakening. I was now a Stranger in a Strange Land and had to puzzle things out. Putting religion to one side, I had accepted there was some sort of creator.

If **that** was true, then perhaps I had a **Soul**! The concept of an immortal Soul is something I have always struggled with. If it's immortal, then where does it come from when you're born? **Surely it must already exist**.

Where and what was it doing before I was born? I'd been conditioned into believing that reincarnation was simply an aspect of faith-based religions and not real. Now I was no longer so sure, but most of what I was reading about the subject was religious and just didn't resonate as mostly True.

As a child, my mother was fond of telling me the legend of Robert the Bruce and his observation of a spider struggling to spin its web. It kept trying. It never gave up. Eventually it succeeded.

I remember thinking back then that I would be the same. I would keep trying until I succeeded. Every failure would be a lesson learned. Every success would be built on a hill of failures. If I chose the wrong path, I would try a different one.

This was conditioning, another belief, but it's one that felt true and still does.

My inquiries led me to numerous guru's and spiritual writers. I was consuming essays and Youtube videos whenever I had the time. Much of it was resonating, but a lot of it wasn't.

It took a while before I realised, they were aimed at the un-enlightened. Do this, practise that, deny yourself this, attend this workshop or subscribe to this program and the path to enlightenment will be found.

It was Saviour complex stuff and I realised I didn't want to be led by anyone anywhere anymore. That was the trap I'd walked into blindly as a child, deferring to people in Authority. Not again.

I felt stuck. I had little difficulty perceiving what was False (almost everything) but how could I find what was True? Was that even possible when so much misinformation and disinformation was everywhere?

The process of Inquiry reveals the Gordian Knot nature of reality. There are so many layers, so many theories, that it

seems impossible to unravel the twisted coils and get to the core understandings.

Who am I? Why am I here? Why have I no memory of anything before this Life? These are the core questions and the most important, but what I found online wasn't answering these.

I could read all I wanted to about conspiracy theories, but they weren't dealing with the core questions.

What could I do differently? I was going sideways not forward. What else could I do? If I possessed a Soul, did I have a Spirit Guide? It was outside the box! How could I reach out to it?

The next thing I knew I was buying a pendulum and 'talking' to my Guide(s) and Higher Self.

"Nothing can come of nothing".

I didn't feel I was being reckless. I've risked my Life in countless ways over the years doing ladder work and chatting to some spirits wasn't daunting. I did take some precautions and read quite a lot of guidance before attempting to make contact, but then I did.

My pendulum experience began with me reading about using one online. I visited some paranormal websites and read various testaments from people who had contacted their guides. I bought a pendulum, printed out a sheet of paper with some letters and numbers on it and gave it a go.

I started by clearing my house of negative influences. This was done by deliberately rotating the pendulum clockwise while silently reciting an intention to clear my house of all negative energy or entities.

I would then ask a series of Yes/No questions to which the pendulum would either move left to right (No) forward and backward (Yes) or circle counter clockwise (Don't know / Can't say).

The first few questions I would already know the answer to, to validate the veracity of the answers. I didn't have to ask the questions audibly. Directing the questions mentally was enough.

The movements were subtle, but they were there! It was really weird, made all the weirder by some of the answers I got. One of my earliest was to ask if 'are all my thoughts my own?' **No!**

I could **not** believe the answer, it was mad and disturbing, but then as I sat and calmly observed the thoughts that came into my mind, I realised - Fuck! It **was** true. This knowledge was/is important.

Just as importantly was the origin of the question. Why had I asked that particular question? As I reflected upon it, much later, I realised the question had come from nowhere!

I did some stupid things, like asking for and getting the winning lottery numbers – except they weren't. Not even close Lol. I'd imagined winning enough money to flee to some remote location taking my whole extended family with me.

It was an important lesson that I needed to learn. Whatever my destiny was, that wasn't it and whatever my Guides purpose was, it wasn't to assist me in cheating fate.

In the first few months of communicating with my guides they gave me valuable insights in terms of lines of inquiry, which could be followed. Books worth reading where Truth was hiding in amongst Lies.

This all began towards the end of June 21. We were coming out of another lockdown and the national vaccination programme was in full swing. I was not enjoying work and the Spirit World was a welcome distraction.

I do remember at the time chatting to one of my customers who was living in a mobile home. It was a lovely sunny day. He needed a couple of slabs re-laying on his path. He looked ill, very frail, but only about ten years older than me.

He explained that he'd asked me to help because he was terminally ill – cancer. I asked him if he'd tried any alternative therapies like spiritual healing? He shook his head slowly and said he wasn't interested. He'd made peace with it.

He went on to ask if I'd read any of the works of T Lobsang Rampa – the Mad Monk? 'No, I hadn't'. He told me he was a fraud and a charlatan, who he'd come across when he'd spent time in India. He was still interesting though.

That was all he had to say. I thought no more of it except I did feel admiration for his stoicism and hoped I would display the same in similar circumstances. I asked my guides who directed me to which of the Mad Monk books to buy.

His stories contained many truths, in the same way a play by Shakespeare confers fundamental truths we all recognise. Tibet was / is a very special place but in many ways it's just the same as everywhere else.

A few days later and we got away to our static caravan on the coast for a break, except instead it went to another level of weirdness. I noticed my whole body was shaking. As soon as I sat down or stood still, I could sense it. It would come and go in intensity. It wouldn't go away and made it difficult to sleep.

I've had irregular sleep patterns for years where I'd be waking up every night around 1.30 am for an hour or so before going back to sleep. This pattern would last for about a month and then back to normal before starting again.

This was **different**. I was **feeling** something, and it **wasn't** going away. At the time I was paranoid I was infected with some sort of Demon, and I was feeling its struggles to stay attached to me. I still have no idea what was causing it.

The shaking peaked after a couple of days and nights with no sleep. At around 3 in the morning the shaking became so intense it felt like there was electricity bouncing around inside me.

In desperation I went outside barefoot, stamping around on the grass trying to ground myself. After a while something happened, and I just felt freezing cold and weak. I struggled back into the caravan and crawled into bed.

As I lay on my back trying to process what was happening, I felt something **new**. I felt Love or at least a feeling of warmth, pleasure, caring, and approval that was flowing in a stream through the ceiling and down into my Heart.

It kept coming and coming. It was flowing into me and around me. I couldn't see it, but I could **feel** it. It was an incredible feeling that words cannot accurately convey. I snuggled up to Lesley and encouraged the stream of Love to wrap around us like a cocoon and fell into a dreamless sleep.

We returned home the following day, and my guides agreed that I buy more pendulums – around half a dozen of them -

quartz, smokey quartz, rose quartz, jade, and a couple of others. They told me which ones to buy. I was directed to spin them over a glass of water, while clearing my mind.

I would then drink the water and repeat. Sometimes just one pendulum, sometimes a combination of three or more successively. I did this perhaps a hundred times over the next couple of weeks. I didn't notice any effects.

I was encouraged to meditate, and they endorsed me using the hemi sync tapes from the Monroe institute. I liked the idea of being able to Astral travel so I could meet my guides in person and the tapes could enable this.

The tapes certainly had effects, but to date I have not been able to consciously Astral travel. Some of us can, some of us can't. Although **all of us** Astral travel in our Dreams.

Besides using the Monroe tapes, I also read his books and the declassified US military report on his techniques. I recommend you do the same if you haven't come across Robert Monroe before.

This was a tricky time for me psychologically. It was easy to imagine that something magical was taking place (it was) and it was going to lead to some sort of transformation, but the nature of it was veiled to me.

I imagined that I would develop supernatural powers and be able to manipulate reality. I'd be able to render all weapons inoperable and other wishful fantasies. Thankfully nothing like that manifested, so fortunately I wasn't capable of interfering with anything.

The Saviour complex is a clever one. If we can't find a saviour, we aspire to be one, but it's like most other conditioned beliefs – cobblers. I did have the sense that I'd begun something and now just wanted to progress as far as I could. I tried to put all my fantasies to one side.

I felt like I needed to do a lot of inner work to progress, which I did, but I didn't recognise the work I'd already done to get me to this point. Consequently, it felt like I was just starting, and this gave me a sense of excitement and an appetite to learn more.

Robert Monroe's descriptions of reincarnation on Earth were credible, non-religious, and resonated with me as mostly true. It was clear he believed in his expanded view of reality based on his personal experiences over many years.

It had never made him fabulously rich or famous and I couldn't detect a hidden agenda, although I doubt, he revealed everything he experienced and learned. His revelations were more science fiction than spiritual.

I understood his words, but understanding and knowing are not the same thing and I was lacking the direct personal experience he'd had. My inability to replicate them was frustrating.

After reflecting on it a thought came into my mind. You've only looked at fairly recent information in your inquiries – why not go further back?

I'd start studying the Occult i.e. The Hidden Knowledge.

Occult simply means **hidden.** The Dark connotations associated with the word are simply there to keep them that way - hidden. With more of my fears gone, I saw no logical reason for not studying the subject. It might have turned out to be nonsense, but if I didn't even look, I'd never **know**.

"The Principles of Truth are Seven; he who knows these, understandingly, possesses the Magic Key before whose touch all the Doors of the Temple fly open."

It's more sci-fi than divine.

I studied and / or practised to some degree:

The Hermetic Principles, Tarot, Crystals, Spiritism, Spirituality, Shamanism, Qi Gong, Taoism, Biogeometry, Sacred and Infernal Geometry, Quantum theory, Terrain theory, Germ theory, Tartaria and other historical revisionism, Gnosticism, The Psychonaut Robert Monroe, Q Posts, Symbolism, Holographic Universe, Gematria, Pythagorean Numerology, Past Life regression, Hidden power structures, Herbalism, Orgone generators, Meditation, Yogic breathing, and Astrology.

It's not an exhaustive list, I've probably missed referencing other things.

My approach was to study everything that arose, but particularly those things taught in the Mystery Schools. This was (allegedly) where the Elites in the older times were educated in the **secret** teachings that were reserved for them. They still are within certain organisations.

I came close to joining one of the orders that exists today, but on reflection decided not to. I've become averse to being led by anyone or anything apart from my higher self.

We are **programmed** to avoid the occult. That what keeps it hidden. Like everything else it is in **plain sight**. No-one is prevented from finding them if they look, although you do have to look hard.

Although the Hermetic Principles are not the oldest occult knowledge, they are attributed to Hermes Trismegistus who was thought to have lived around 400 BC, so pretty ancient. I found them mind stretching.

The Seven Hermetic Principles seek to explain **Everything**, which is a **big** task. I find their meanings sink a little deeper into my mind every time I focus my attention of them. I suspect the same will be true in the future as they reveal more and more. Here is my interpretation of The Hermetic Principles:

1. The Principle of Mentalism

The Universe is Mental. You can say that again! Except it doesn't mean that the World is insane (even if it is). It means that at the fundamental base level, it is **made of thought** or **consciousness**.

The **deception** we are conditioned to accept is that **God** is somehow **somewhere else**. Whether it's a bloke with a Beard on a cloud, or something only accessible through prayer, meditation, or contemplation, as **He** isn't here all the time. But **He is**.

Think about it. Where does all the stuff that **isn't** God come from, unless you accept the obvious, which is that everything **is** God. That includes you, me and Haribos. **Everything.**

Once I comprehended that, the next stage was recognising that Everything is made of the same essential stuff. My physical body is around 70% water, plus some minerals. In turn these are made of atoms.

The atoms are made of electrical charges – positive, negative, and neutral. None of which have much mass. Keep blowing the atoms to bits it's more of the same, although they're now called quarks or bosons or charms. It goes on and on.

What the principle of Mentalism tells us, is that when someone does finally get to the essential nature of reality, they'll find it's all the same. A unified and unbroken field of consciousness. For me, this is logical and inescapable.

God is not somewhere else, but everywhere - and God is **All things**. God is the source of everything, whatever we perceive to be good **OR** bad **is** God. We are **all** part of God. God is **unknowable** and just is.

Not what most **Religions** teach is it? I wonder why?

2. The Principle of Correspondence

"As above, so below; as within, so without."

Everything is connected, and in many ways the illusion that everything is made up of **different** things is explained by this principle. Everything is also subdivided into planes. There is the material plane, the mental plane, the astral plane and more. Our thoughts in the mental plane, manifest themselves in the material plane. For instance, you **think** about going to the shop **before** you go there.

What you feel on the inside reflects what you see on the outside. They correspond with each other.

3. The Principle of Vibration

"Nothing rests; everything moves; everything vibrates."

This is very clever as it allows God to be efficient when it comes to organising everything. Large chunks are vibrating differently. This means (like radio waves) they can all occupy the same space but be invisible to each other.

Everything vibrates – this includes not just our physical bodies and the material World, but our emotions as well. The lowest emotional vibration is Fear. The highest is thought to be Unconditional Compassion.

4. The Principle of Polarity

"Everything is Dual; everything has poles; everything has its pair of opposites; like and unlike are the same; opposites are identical in nature, but different in degree; extremes meet; all truths are but half-truths; all paradoxes may be reconciled."

Living on Earth is a great place to learn about polarity. We are conditioned to believe that polarity is simply about positive v negative, hot v cold, good v bad, but as I'll explain it's not as simple as that.

For example, Wealth v Poverty. Can you point to an income and say this is the exact middle? No. Can you have one without the other. No. Without poverty, no-one would be wealthy and vice versa.

This also means that everything is **the same** to some degree or other and that everything is both partly true and partly false. Can you understand how extreme wealth and extreme poverty could be the same thing?

Then there's extreme agony and extreme ecstasy, are they the same? Extreme Left v Extreme Right, is there a discernible difference?

Knowledge only exists because of Ignorance, Freedom because of Slavery. Opposites are polarity expressions of the same thing and paradoxical.

Clever, isn't it?

5. The Principle of Rhythm

"Everything flows, out and in; everything has its tides; all things rise and fall; the pendulum-swing manifests in everything; the measure of the swing to the right is the measure of the swing to the left; rhythm compensates."

Deep down, we all know this to be true, but we are conditioned against applying it. **Birth, Growth, Maturity, Decay, Death**. This is the process that governs our existence and that of all material life. We are conditioned to celebrate and enjoy the first half, then deny and avoid the second half.

There is a rhythm to everything. Being sensitive to these rhymes enables you to anticipate what might unfold. The rhymes can measure in hours, days, weeks, years, decades, centuries, millennia and beyond.

There are rhythms to our emotional state, becoming aware of these and taking control of them is found on the path to achieving balance. Even so, I'm no expert!

6. The Principle of Cause and Effect

"Every Cause has its Effect; every Effect has its Cause; everything happens according to Law; Chance is but a name for Law not recognized; there are many planes of causation, but nothing escapes the Law."

Everyone has heard of it, but **very few** understand it. We are conditioned to think the idea that **everything** has meaning is the stuff of psychosis. It's one of the most important gate keepers of the conditioned mind.

An Awakening individual becomes consciously aware that for a significant proportion of their Life, they were not fully consciously aware.

At the time they **believed** they were consciously aware, but a perception shift has revealed to them that they were not.

This is clearly an **effect**, but was the **cause**? It must have had one, perhaps more than one.

Also, you discover that there are many other people who've all experienced this same effect. Some recently, others long ago. All of us become Strangers in a Strange land. After this kind of Awakening, it is not possible to view reality as simply random events.

Everything you do, say, or think has an effect. By being mindful of your thoughts and actions, you can move from being an Actor to an Observer. Doing nothing may seem to be a safe course, but inaction may still be the cause of something else.

7. The Principle of Gender

"Gender is in everything; everything has its Masculine and Feminine Principles; Gender manifests on all planes."

Putting the sexual context of Masculine and Feminine to one side and just focusing on the **archetypal nature** of gender is how to understand the principle of Gender.

In the case of a Man there resides within both an aggressive aspect and a nurturing aspect. Within a Woman it is a nurturing aspect and an aggressive aspect. Everything reflects the dualities of the masculine and feminine, but in varying degrees.

I've used the example of a Human because it's a clear one, but you can apply this principle to an apple or a rock.

None of these principles are religious. They acknowledge the existence of a creator, and its nature as we perceive it. Its everything and everywhere. God is always present, cannot be lost, cannot be found.

I'm very conscious of Cause and Effect. It was obviously something I recognised from before Awakening, but not its all-encompassing application. I now try to remember to turn my Attention up to maximum as situations arise.

All these words are a consequence of Cause and Effect and who knows what Effect they might Cause. I've examined my motivation to write them and I'm content that my intention is to do no harm.

All the principles are a very different way of looking at reality and our place within it. I cannot say they are absolutely true, but my discernment tells me that they are more true than false.

They are not a Belief system, because their Truth is discernible, and their understanding transcends all beliefs. At least that is the position with which I view them nowadays.

Every time I think I understand them, I realise I don't. For instance, a man who possesses all Knowledge is at the extreme of that polarity. Therefore, he also knows nothing. The fruits of the principles are paradoxes.

It hasn't stopped me digging deeper though as I have the conviction that there was / is something else. A deeper meaning behind this experience **beyond** declaring it as being just that it is what it is.

While the Hermetic Principles promise the resolution of all paradoxes I came to an important understanding. **They only apply within this version of reality**. As such they **could** be described as a deception, but a revealing one.

"Fortune brings in some boats that are not steered".

According to the 7 Hermetic principles, **there is no such thing as absolute Truth**. Everything is partly true and partly false but finding out that most of what I formerly believed was mostly false, it was reasonable to explore what might be **mostly** true or at least only partly false.

I consulted a Tarot reader, which is something I never dreamed I would ever do. I found her online and made an appointment, she lived just a few miles away. The reader was a friendly middle-aged lady who had a room in her house set aside as a sacred place.

She told me I was lost and looking for direction – true. I was receiving many downloads from my higher self, which can be overwhelming. I did feel overwhelmed. I asked her why I was only Awakening now. Why not before?

She told me that it was simply the right time. Had I begun Awakening twenty years ago I wouldn't have been ready. This was also true. I was now being **tested**, but the future looked good. Really good.

The session concluded. You might think I would feel really positive about what I'd been told, but at the time I felt mainly disappointment. I was being tested! **WTF!** Hadn't I suffered enough?

Apparently not. There was more to come. By this time, I knew that my only way forward was to surrender to whatever higher forces were directing my Life and stop fighting them, but old habits die hard.

My Pendulum then informed me of a shattering revelation. I was not who I thought I was as a Human. I'd been switched at birth for another child (by accident). I'm a twin, so this was highly unlikely, although an unidentical one, so possible.

I was given my biological brother's name and told that he was living in the US.

Despite my scepticism I investigated, even engaging a genealogist to see if there was any truth to this revelation. As far as I could tell, no other twins were born in the Hospital where I was around the same time.

However, when I asked my Mum about her recollections, she told me another mother had given birth to twins the night before we were delivered. There was no official record of this happening, which was a puzzle. Had she mis-remembered?

My genealogist also confirmed that no-one existed with the name I'd been given. I felt such a fool. Why had I even entertained the notion? My Mother's recollections were incorrect. There was no other credible explanation.

As a child I'd been teased by my brothers that I was an orphan, and it obviously settled into my psyche as a trigger, otherwise I wouldn't have remembered it. This debacle had been fuelled by an unresolved childhood trauma. I understood. I let the trauma dissolve and resolved not make the same mistake again.

It had been a test. The Tarot reader had tried to tell me……

I think I first came across Dolores Cannon on Youtube. She died over a decade ago, but her legacy is considerable. Her story was that of a hypnotherapist who specialised in past life regression. She did this thousands of times with different subjects.

I found one of her practitioners a 30 min drive away and booked a session.

Up until my Awakening I was convinced that I was one of those people who could not be hypnotised. Lol. I **knew** differently now.

My first regression took me into what seemed 18th century England, and I was a thirty-year-old country gentleman. In the regression I thrashed a stable boy with a walking stick. There was no justification, I'd flown into a rage over some imagined slight.

The look in the boy's eyes cut into me. I felt his pain, I could see he was innocent. I felt ashamed. In hurting him, I had hurt myself. I felt terrible and understood why I was being shown this scene.

The next was about a century later. I was at the opening of a railway station in the countryside. It was a celebration. Again, I seemed to be a bit of a somebody. People were congratulating me. The railway was going to change everything.

I didn't share their excitement but pretended to. The station would not last, nor the railway. It was no more permanent than the cow sheds that had stood where the station was now built. Nothing lasts, everything changes. All victories are hollow, all defeats are meaningless. I understood.

I didn't really know what to expect when I was hypnotised. I was hoping for something more, something direct and logical, but had no idea what that might be. Instead, I had an experience that related to the Hermetic principles, which was curious.

Pythagorean Numerology was/is ancient knowledge as well, so I started studying it. It helped me look at things in a different way and I was able to apply it to some difficult challenges, which made life easier to navigate.

The main challenge it revealed that I would be facing through 2022-23, was standing up for myself. I thought I'd already done this by refusing the vaccine, but that was the year before, so didn't know what it meant.

In the past I'd often found myself in personal situations where I felt compelled to do something against my better judgement. I would complain, argue, and procrastinate, but ultimately submit.

I recognised that these scenarios had repeated over the years with always the same outcome. I would complain but submit. Next time it arose I would behave differently. I would not complain or procrastinate. I would just state my position and stick to it and see if it changed the outcome.

Out of the blue, a situation arose. Despite being prepared for its arrival I could easily have behaved the same as I had in the past, I very nearly did, but I didn't. I won't go into the details except to say that I passed the test. At least I think I did. Lol

I undertook around 30 Numerology profiles of people I already knew, including my own and they provided valuable insights about what I didn't know about them **and** myself. It changed my opinions about all of them including me.

I noted my next challenge involved developing my artistic talents and being of service to humanity. Despite all the evidence I'd gathered from learning and applying numerology I dismissed this as complete bollocks.

Me? An Artist? I struggle to paint a wall evenly (I don't like decorating!) and while I think I can compose a photo adequately; I didn't consider myself as being artistic in any meaningful way.

Then in early 2023 I started writing. Shit!

I've never really felt like shaking my fist at the sky and screaming fuck you as loud as I can, although it was there, lurking in my shadow side. It didn't make any difference how I felt about it. It was what it was, might as well embrace it.

I began to suspect that everything we perceive, and experience is described by Numbers. It's unbelievable and obvious. I'm not saying that Pythagorean Numerology is the key – I think it's deeper and more complex than that as you'll see.

There are other veils to penetrate. For all I know the veils continue indefinitely. For me, this brought a new kind of understanding, it's not about reaching a particular destination but the journey itself.

I didn't feel the need to sell all my possessions and go to Tibet or anything similar, because I was exploring a World that was already present. It is **within me** and **you as well**.

Our World exists in two ways. There is the Exoteric (external) and Esoteric (internal) Worlds.

The Exoteric is the World as it is, the Esoteric is as we perceive it internally, which we then project outward as our external reality. For some people the World is full of joy and laughter, for others it is full of horror and fear. It's the **same** World.

The Principle of Correspondence explains this – As Above, So Below, As Within, So Without.

It is only by going within and examining our thoughts, biases, beliefs, and memories that we can start to take control of our perceptions. Before doing this, we are simply reacting to external stimuli instinctively without questioning where those instincts and beliefs originate.

This is a challenging concept, made even more difficult by the fact that we don't fully perceive the Exoteric World in the first place, because we don't sense all of it. We only perceive that which we pay **attention** to.

I've lost count of the number of times I've injured myself working where I had no idea that I was cut and bleeding until

I saw the blood. My **attention** was elsewhere. Whatever your **attention** is focussed on will **dominate** your perception.

When I pay attention to pain, I feel it. When I pay attention to something else to the point where it totally absorbs me, the pain disappears (until I pay attention to it again). Interesting, isn't it? I have Tinnitus, but most of the time I don't notice it, although it's **always** there.

Your interaction with other Humans is both an exoteric and esoteric process and a critical aspect of your learning experience. Isolating yourself from others, particularly unconscious people, may feel necessary but it isn't. In fact, it may be counter-productive, but you must do what you must do to keep your sanity.

It seems that many Awakening people go through a period of isolation, so if this applies to you, don't feel surprised or bad about it.

Paying **ATTENTION** to what you experience for me was the key to understanding the meaning behind what otherwise may appear to be random or chance events.

One of the **most** helpful techniques I've learned is to **mentally replay my day in reverse**. If you struggle with **insomnia** this can be a very useful tool. As you settle down to sleep, you replay your actions in reverse e.g. The time you spent in the Bathroom, the time you spent getting undressed, the route you took to your Bedroom, the programme you were watching/listening to before you turned off the TV or the Radio or the Book you were reading, whatever came before that and then before that etc.

Do this and you will fall asleep, but before you do, you will notice things that weren't apparent at the time, particularly interactions with others. If I recall it in the third person, rather than POV, it allows me to observe myself.

After a few goes you'll notice something. You'll notice that you're thinking about things in a very different way. I'm no expert at it - I'm still learning but if you sincerely try it, I'm confident you'll see.

My experiments with contacting my Guides had revealed something to me about the spirit realm. It was the same as the material realm – full of disinformation, or as I call them, mischievous bastards.

This was consistent with the principle of correspondence. As Above, So Below.

I asked my Guides how I could overcome this, and the response was emphatic – **meditation**. I groaned inwardly. I've always found it difficult to relax and sitting around humming was not something I felt would work, but ultimately, I found a way.

For me (and this is my personal experience) I started by deciding on a question or problem that I wanted to pursue and writing it on a piece of paper. I then sit in a chair, close my eyes, and focus on my breathing.

I try not to think about anything and any thoughts that do arise are acknowledged and allowed to go on their way. After about ten minutes I begin to perceive behind my closed eyes what appears to be a clear Blue sky.

It is at this point I recall the question or problem that I've written down and deliberately think it in my mind. I'll spend a few minutes more enjoying the moment, then open my eyes and get on with my day.

The answer to my question or problem will generally present itself within a day or so of the meditation – provided I'm paying attention. It will come as a result of a seemingly random interaction with someone, or an article, or book, even something on the TV – like Magic, because it **is** Magic.

If I'm unable to think of anything specific, I just ask that whatever I need to know or would be useful to me at this time would be welcome.

I'm sure someone will disagree with my method, tell me my 'Blue sky' is a result of phosphenes reacting when my eyes close, or scold me that I should meditate every day, not just when I feel inclined to do so.

I don't really care what other people's opinions are, **only** that of my higher self. I may not know exactly who or what I am, but I know **I am** and inquiring into the nature of that **I am** was the next step in my inquiries.

If someone were to die while being simultaneously weighed, no matter how sensitive the scales, they would not register any difference. This is a real mystery. Anyone who has seen a dead body, particularly of someone they knew when they were alive, will understand this.

Something has gone. What was it? Where does it go? Where does it originate? These are questions that have frustrated and obsessed many great thinkers and philosophers.

Most thinkers either decide it's Nothing or it's the Soul. There isn't any middle ground, except from my inquiries there is another explanation. What disappears is the animating force - Spirit, the Subtle or Etheric body.

My inquiries turned towards understanding what it is.

"Each separate being in the universe returns to the common source."

Cosmologists agree that there is something acting upon the Universe that cannot be seen or detected. The term Dark Energy has been used to describe these unseen phenomena. It makes up around 70% of everything according to those who developed the hypothesis.

The point here is that there is mainstream acceptance that there is **more** to reality than we can see.

What if it could be detected or at least perceived by some people?

There are numerous references by different cultures going back into antiquity about Subtle or Etheric Energy:

The Etheric energy is part of the source consciousness from which everything is manifested. I refer to it as **Subtle** because it is. So subtle, that for most of us, we are oblivious to its existence, even though I suspect we use it and sense it **all the time**.

In **addition** to your physical body, you have a non-physical subtle body. Both occupy the same time and space as each other, but your subtle body extends beyond the physical form by some distance.

There are numerous individuals who can perceive the subtle bodies of others. They're described as being able to see a person's Aura. I'm not one of them, but having researched the subject, I don't believe they're making it up.

The centre of the subtle body is located near your Heart. Were you able to see it with your physical eyes the Heart vortex or Chakra would appear to be a wafer-thin horizontally rotating disc of pure energy, around 7" in diameter with a greenish colouration. You would also be able to see that is just one of hundreds of whirling energy vortexes that are distributed throughout your subtle body, which in turn are aligned with aspects of the physical body.

There are 7 main vortexes or Chakras that align with the central nervous system and are distributed from the top of the skull to the base of the spine. Collectively they form the core of the subtle body and from which they create a bioenergetic field. Each Chakra has its own colour, from Red at the Base Chakra to Violet at the Crown Chakra, just like the spectrum of light.

This field is much larger than the physical body and can extend at least 10 metres in all directions. It interacts with other fields as it moves around; other Humans, other life forms and the planet itself.

You are instinctively sensitive to these other fields. It's why your feet know where the ground is without having to look exactly where they're being placed. It's also why you can sense if you're being watched and why you can get a good or bad vibe from certain people or places.

You learned how to do all this before you could talk and can't remember what it was like before you could. It's a completely natural and integrated aspect of every one of us.

We don't need to think about breathing or digesting food, the body just gets on with it thanks to the sympathetic nervous system, although sometimes you'll notice it you burp or fart!

The subtle body does what it does without us being consciously aware as well. When it does get through to our conscious mind, it's often with a physical feeling. Goose bumps, flash of reflux, feeling watched. These are examples and everyone is different.

Without your subtle body, your physical body would be dead. It is the Life force that animates the flesh. Every living organism on the planet is animated by this Life force. Dogs have Chakras and a subtle body as well (in case you wondered) as have all other life forms to a greater or lesser extent.

You can detect these energy fields in a variety of ways e.g. Dowsing, but they all involve direct personal experience. The first time I became consciously aware of subtle energy was during and after some exercises with pendulums. I could **feel** subtle vibrations through the pendulum chains.

According to the teachings your bioenergetic field is not your Soul, but it **is** the life force that animates your physical body. The Soul is something else entirely and supposedly not even **here** although you are **permanently** connected to it.

Your field both receives and transmits energy. It's been described as energetically leaky or porous. Stuff goes in and stuff comes out. We are all conditioned to believe that all our thoughts are our own. After all we **hear** them in our own voice.

This is more **false** than true, although **some** of our thoughts are self-generated, from my own observations, it appears quite a few **aren't**.

Mozart credited the Divine for his musical compositions. He didn't know where his ideas came from, but he knew which notes followed the preceding ones as if they were completely obvious.

Once you accept that thoughts can originate elsewhere, you can start to apply discernment to them and decide whether they are internally or externally generated, positive, negative, or neutral.

Even the words on this page should not be attributed solely to the genius and wisdom of the author.

Within this unseen realm, parasites feed on Human emotional energy. Some attach themselves permanently if they get the opportunity.

Unless you're able to discriminate between your thoughts you will undoubtedly have succumbed to the "I know I should not do this, but I am going to do it anyway" insanity that often precedes the **stupid** mistakes we make.

Thoughts can be inserted by a parasite to engineer an emotional output. If we **learn** from those experiences, then the parasite has served a useful purpose.

If we don't, we are inclined to **repeat** the experience and the parasite starts feeling at home. This is where a parasite can take up permanent residence. Why wouldn't they? We are their food source.

Another obvious example is road rage. Some people become enraged while driving and become incredibly aggressive. Here the parasites don't hang around, but will move on once they've fed.

Once you recognise these sorts of thoughts for what they are, you can **examine** and **discard** them. Then the gaps in your shield should begin to **heal** up. You are encouraged to be **mindful of your thoughts**. **You can't control them arising**, but you **can choose** whether to entertain them or not.

Thoughts are not bad or good, they are just thoughts. I suffered for many years with the belief that all my thoughts were my own, because like everyone, I had some bad thoughts. So bad, there's no way I'd repeat them here!

I now **know**, having practised mindfulness sincerely and regularly, that my thoughts really do come from **nowhere** and it's surprising how few are consciously generated.

I'm driving in the van. I'm passing Morrisons. **Why don't I pop in and pick up some milk and a bunch of flowers for Lesley.** I've got 2 seconds to make up my mind. I **like** this thought. Indicator on, filter onto the slip road.

I'm sitting in front of the laptop thinking about another example. Instead, my thoughts ask me if I should get another cup of tea. My back sends a signal, HEY I'm aching. I realise these are just thoughts and let them go.

Another thought tells me that I'm wasting my time writing these words. No-one will read them, so what's the point? Rather than get into an argument with my thought, I let it go and carry on writing.

If I have a thought that I'm somehow better than the un-awakening people – I can recognise that it's arrogant and false, so I let it go. There are days when I feel frustration or a sense of failure, but these things are simply thoughts, so I try to let them pass and remember that I like Awakening and I'm patient.

All Spiritual teachings put emphasis on unblocking and balancing the Chakras. The Chakras act as gates within your core energetic field. They can be open or shut. When shut they will restrict the flow of energy through the Kundalini. The Kundalini is the looped energetic highway connecting all the 7 Chakras from bottom to top and vice versa.

The top or 7th Chakra leads to your direct connection to your higher self or Soul.

Chakras can get shut or heavily restricted as a defence mechanism and there is always some sort of trauma at its core.

Trauma doesn't necessarily mean dramatic. Our conditioning damage is mainly done before we can even properly speak, usually by the actions of parents who are trying their best to raise a demanding baby.

It's part of the process and every generation is conditioned by the preceding one, although the arrival of mass media has reinforced these inputs on an industrial scale, as has the Education system.

If you (like me) are a parent, this is a horrifying realisation and likely to trigger feelings of guilt and horror. **WTF have you done!** The answer is **exactly what you were supposed to do**. It's **not** your fault!

Whatever you might have done is a consequence of conditioning you received from your parents. In my own case I can remember deciding when I became a father that I would be different to my own parents.

Everything I hated about how they brought me up, I would not repeat, and for the most part I was successful. It meant my kids had a different childhood than me, but I can't say it was a better or happier one.

Dealing with these traumas and blockages and your inner Demons is called Shadow Work, and as far as I can tell, you can never complete it. This doesn't necessarily mean going into a deep meditation, but it does mean confronting your beliefs, eventually **all** of them.

Most of us are blind to our blockages. It's easier to ignore than confront them. This wilful blindness is what keeps us imprisoned, which is very clever.

Your energetic field has a vibration, which fluctuates based on your emotional state. At the lowest level is Fear. At the highest level is Unconditional Compassion for Everything.

Anger is **above** Fear, so has a higher vibration. **This is an important understanding**. For anyone consciously wanting to raise their vibration, they might consider looking at the small steps. They are easier than leaping straight to the top of the Tower.

It was Anger that was my dominating emotions when my Awakening was triggered, but it was controlled anger, not blind and explosive.

There is a lot to learn on this subject and lots of sources and resources. I would encourage you to read and explore as much as you wish.

I understand now how beliefs govern your perception of reality as they dictate what your Ego can or cannot accept. All your biases and beliefs are a function of your programming and it's a kind of psychological death to let go of all your beliefs and become open to looking at reality in a new way.

Some teachers refer to this as Ego death, but (in my experience) it isn't. Your Ego **does** survive the process but, consequently it'll become different. The objective is to embody your **true** nature, and this is challenging.

To progress it was **necessary to forgive myself** for anything I regretted doing prior to Awakening. This was not easy even though I was not aware I was Asleep at the time.

I found this **very** difficult. We are conditioned that 'Ignorance is No Defence".

This is more false than true given that we are ignorant of our reason for being here. I've consoled myself that no-one stands a chance. It's like giving a blind child a 1000-piece jigsaw puzzle and criticising them for not getting it right.

Guilt is a difficult blockage. As is Greed. As is Envy. As is Self-Pity. As is Blaming others, as is Fear. Not just Fear of dying, but of ridicule, embarrassment, failure, the list goes on and on. **To progress I had to confront all of these**.

This was daunting – and still is, but I discovered something that helped me enormously. Everything we do, say or think is **recorded** in a non-physical location known as the Akashic records. **Everything.**

One of my most difficult blockages was Guilt. I've done so many stupid things in my Life that it would take another two books to list them all. No matter how hard I wish they hadn't happened, they happened.

According to many teachings, when the physical body dies, the subtle body will go to the Akashic records for a replay of this Life, and it will **ALL** be waiting for them to be replayed. I suspect anyone else who's interested will be able to see it as well. Enough said. **God knows everything.** We have **no** secrets.

According to many teachings there is a direct link between the Health of the Physical body and that of the Subtle body. You are what you **think** as well as what you eat. The Placebo effect is the clearest demonstration that the mind directly effects the physical body, both positively and negatively.

Your subtle body is connected to and part of the Planetary Morphogenetic field. The Soul resides elsewhere but is permanently connected to the subtle body via an energetic cord between the two.

The Soul can be referred to as your higher self or whatever you feel comfortable referring to it as. Just as your subtle body is not quite your Human form, your Soul has a different form as well. It doesn't really matter what it looks like, it's more powerful and capable than our limited imaginations can stretch.

It is Ageless and Genderless. It has **all** the knowledge of your countless incarnations. When the physical body dies, this understanding is imparted to you as you merge into and become one with it. Your consciousness **lives on**, but in a vastly expanded state.

It is unencumbered by the belief systems that are programmed into us as Humans. It's the silent observer of our existence, only giving us a nudge when we need it. Our **core** personality, **without** the layers of conditioning, is an authentic version of your Soul persona.

You may sense that your true nature is one of being of service to others. Alternatively, you may sense that your true calling is to be selfish and self-centred. There is no right or wrong in this, you are whatever you are.

The important part is identifying the parts of your personality that are an **act**.

Sounds easy, but when you discount your age, gender, orientation, job, family, hobbies, politics, and memories, there's not a lot left! I'm still not sure what the authentic me is, but I like to think my sense of humour is the real me.

I would certainly encourage all readers to explore the hidden World of subtle energy. When you experience its effects, your mind may want to reject it. I did and I think it's one of the defence mechanisms programmed into us.

Spirituality fails to address the reality of our lives as hypnotised slaves, in the same way that Religion ignores it completely as well. In addition, many practitioners set themselves up as leadership figures and it all seems to get quasi-religious. My own case of Awakening occurred without having done any sort of recognised Spiritual practice.

I managed to get enough of my fears under control and angry enough to pierce the veil and (as Tommy Cooper would say) 'just like that'. I was Awakening.

For a long time, I failed to fully recognise the significance of my Awakening experience. Some Asleep people work for years on a spiritual path looking to become enlightened and a lot of what's out there as Spirituality, is aimed at **them**.

They should be careful what they wish for.

We live in a time of false prophets, who achieve confusion by mixing truths and lies. I've learned much from many of them, but don't follow anyone or any ideology. They're not all bad, but I view everything with scepticism.

The power of the conscious mind to control the Human body has been demonstrated by (among others) Wim Hof, but his is probably the most famous – scaling 24,000 feet of Everest in nothing but shorts, boots, and no oxygen. He turned back 5,000 feet short when he twisted an ankle. Lol

https://www.dailymail.co.uk/news/article-2655008/Dutch-father-five-dubbed-Iceman-turn-thermostat-using-mind-sets-world-record-climbing-Everest-just-shorts.html

This is someone who has control over his physical body by utilising his mental body. His primary message is simple. Take control of your Fears and you can control your physical self, to be superhuman.

For my own part I simply want to see beyond the next veil. I've been fooled into believing in something that I now **know** to be mostly false. I know that the nature of reality as presented to us is a lie, so wtf is it?

'All colours will agree in the Dark'.

What is reality? Contemporary science seems to agree that there's not a lot there. Atoms have virtually no mass. All there seems to be is different energetic charges - positive, negative, and neutral.

Things get even trickier when considering the future and the past. Is there a physical reality within either? The past no longer exists, and the future hasn't happened yet. All we can perceive is the present. So how can it be?

I thought of Holograms being like Princess Leia being projected into the air by R2D2 or in virtual reality scenarios. In these cases, the Holograms are constructed using only visible Light. A subject is observed / recorded from two different angles and the images collected and combined at a single point.

The image produced looks nothing like the original subject, but when projected using two light sources calibrated at the same angles as before, a 3-dimensional image comes into coherent form.

The Electromagnetic and the Sound spectrums are each colossal, but the Holograms we are familiar with use **only visible light**. Imagine that you wanted to record and project other wavelengths, like temperature, sound, even odour and imagine you had a mind the size of the Universe and Eternity?

You could come up with our reality. As each frame unfolds (trillions of times a second) the preceding frame enfolds. This includes all the unseen phenomena that we don't usually perceive. Everything recorded down to the minutest detail.

I've noticed that the words **unfold**, and **unfolding** have become increasingly common when describing events as they occur. I don't know if I've simply become more sensitive to their use or if they actually are, but it's curious that this is exactly how such a simulation would behave – by unfolding.

It would be so clearly real, that to treat reality as a simulation would be considered madness, however this would be a testament to its brilliance rather than a coherent argument against its existence.

As far as I can tell, the entire physical Universe we can see is probably holographic. This position might upset a few Flat Earthers, as it makes their arguments somewhat irrelevant. I have observed large ships disappearing over the horizon on multiple occasions.

This doesn't mean that I **know** that it's a Globe, but I do know that it isn't Flat! Unfortunately, the whole Flat Earth psyop is (in my opinion) a trap and deception. This is primarily because its advocates **believe** it. It's a belief system.

Does it matter if our reality is Holographic? Not particularly, it's still **real**, but Knowledge is Power, and a Holographic Universe still gives limited scope for free – will.

Within such a projection the future might not be entirely fixed. Instead, it is a field of possibilities that crystalize into certainty as the moment of Now approaches.

My limited research of Quantum mechanics led me to the double-slit experiment, where the act of observing affects the result. It's worth looking at as it's one of the few pieces of evidence in the mainstream and its meaning is very significant.

For our Universe to take form it **must** be observed, and this is consistent within a Holographic projection, where **we** are both the projectors **and** receivers!

Can a Universe be both Holographic and Real? Our Universe is as real as real can be. This is just how it's manifested here. It could be different elsewhere and probably is.

If everything is a manifestation of consciousness, then so is a Hologram. That doesn't make it unreal but reveals that someone or something **must** have created it.

Intelligent design is at odds with Evolutionary theory, but if you accept that any Human being is simply the vehicle for **and dependent upon** an immortal soul, Evolutionary theory falls apart as it doesn't recognise this.

I'm not saying that the literal Biblical story of creation is synonymous with Intelligent design, because it isn't. Intelligent design is acknowledging that the entire Universe (not just Earth) was engineered consciously and deliberately.

Someone or something created this environment on purpose, primarily so our immortal souls could experience what it's like to be alive, and what better way of delivering this than allowing a Soul to experience, Birth, Life and Death.

If this is correct, what is running it? A form of Artificial Intelligence beyond our comprehension? It would certainly be a Super Intelligence and if everything is made of consciousness, that includes whatever is running this, artificial or not.

When I first heard of reality being a simulation (long before I began Awakening) my thoughts told me it was impossible. I imagined a large computer with blinking lights within which the simulation was running.

It was preposterous and easily dismissed as fantasy, however I now recognised that this was driven by my biases and beliefs. Whatever might be running the simulation is **beyond** imagination.

The Holographic Universe by Michael Talbot does an excellent job of explaining how our reality could be manifested and its implications, but it doesn't really deal with the biggest question – why does it even exist? For that I tried to think like God.

Clearly, I am not God, I am (hopefully) but a spark of a spark of the creator, so why not give it a go? If you never try, you'll never know. For some reason this was yet another difficult avenue of inquiry.

As soon as I turned my thoughts towards the subject, they would drift towards something else. This alerted me that perhaps I wasn’t as Awakened as I thought I was, or something was still influencing me.

I put it down to my conditioning. From somewhere there was still a voice telling me not to, however I decided to ignore it and see if I was struck by a bolt of lightning.

That hasn’t happened yet.

'Energy is Eternal Delight'

According to the Hermetic Principles, the first principle is that of **Mentalism.** Everything in existence is made of consciousness. This was a difficult concept for me to understand.

If instead of **consciousness** it was all made of **energy** it would have been easier for me to grasp. We are taught Atoms are little more than electrical charge, so in a very real way all **matter** is just a form of energy, but this doesn't make sense when applied to the vacuum of space, where there is no matter.

Consciousness is sometimes confused with self-awareness e.g. conscious vs unconscious but then there's also sub-conscious and super-conscious, so yes, pretty confusing. After meditating on it the following came to me -

Consciousness **is** energy and can be organised into forms that we perceive as Time, Matter **and** Space. The vacuum of Space is a medium through which objects travel and waves of energy like Light. Even in the vacuum of Space there is still **something**. Something undetectable and inexplicable.

If it can be said that if Consciousness comprises **everything,** <u>then</u> everything **is God.** That's all of Time, Space and Matter. I imagined what it must be like to be God and what God was like at the **beginning** or at least when God wasn't so many things.

Shim (She & Him = Shim) is everything **and** self-aware with omnipotence over the **All.** Shim is the **All.** Sounds great, doesn't it? But when I thought about it and if I were God, wouldn't I feel a bit **lonely**? Wouldn't I get bored?

What could I do about it?

From this conundrum **duality** emerges. This is the concept where different things that are made from the same thing (consciousness) are somehow made to **appear** separate from each other.

For instance, **God** takes an element of Shimself and creates an image of Shimself. It is not **God** but a part of the **original God** that now perceives itself as different and 'hey presto' God has a companion. Perhaps **God** decides to create an environment, like a Universe with Galaxies and Solar systems within it, to explore this separation further. Perhaps God makes a copy of shimself that is completely unaware of its origin. Perhaps many copies.

Everything changes all the time and change brings **learning**. When we observe something changing, whether that's external (like a flower growing) or internal (like our understanding about something) we can recognise that there is a meaning to our individual existence.

We might not know what that meaning is, but deep down we all know that we exist and there must be a reason for our existence, a deeper meaning that we're unable to articulate or explain.

This takes us back to the nature of **deception**.

We can all agree that deception is **not** a good thing, but from a different perspective it can be argued that it's not a bad thing either**.** It is only by wholeheartedly **believing** that we are separate and distinct from God and everything else that **we** can learn and grow.

Within the various teachings in Spirituality there appear to be 3 distinct archetypes: The Left Hand, Right Hand and Middle Way with the latter being the obvious (balanced) logical path.

Left = Individual, Right = Unified, Middle = Acknowledging both

I don't know which is the best if any archetype to adopt. I don't resonate with any of them. I **know** I have an individual consciousness, my own personal perception, I also **know** that what I formerly believed to be the physical material World and Universe beyond, is itself an illusion.

That includes the nonphysical aspects as well. The Spirit realm is no more real than the material, just subtler. Therefore, if neither are real or unreal but nevertheless exist to my perception, then it makes sense (to me) to try and balance the material and the nonphysical.

This takes us back to the essential nature of everything and how the separation and differentiation of consciousness is achieved. Like all the answers, when you **get it**, it's obvious. God uses **Numbers.**

"Knowledge itself, is power".

I was never particularly good at Maths. I loved Arithmetic, but never understood Algebra. Whenever I say this in public, someone will volunteer to teach me, which is awkward as I really don't have the motivation to do so. Algebra leaves me cold.

Numbers on the other hand resonate with me and when I learned what I hadn't been taught in school, I discovered that Numbers were **far** more interesting than I'd been led to believe.

There are **only** 9 Numbers, 1-9. **0** isn't a Number. Each Number has **qualities** that are unique to it **AND** these qualities differentiate within the Numbers based on their **polarity** as follows:

1 Initiating, pioneering, leading, independent, individual, original, courageous, mastery, stubborn, ambition, dominance, wilful, selfish. The 1 is rooted in the material, with its top in the Spiritual and symbolises God.

2 Co-operative, adaptable, partner, friendly, harmony, patience, balance, conflicted, dependent, sensitive, over-protective. The 2 is supported by the material, open on one side and symbolises Unity.

3 Expression, communication, sociability, creativity, manifestation, humour, pessimism, exaggeration, foolhardiness, procrastination. The 3 is made up of the upper parts of two 2's and symbolises the connection between God, Spirit, and Man.

4 Foundation, order, growth, practical, constructive, patient, logical, builder, rigid, traditional, responsible, cautious, deprivation, loss. The 4 is the first number that can form a 3-dimensional shape and symbolises the builder of physical reality. It also looks like a House.

5 Vision, freedom, change, variety, analytical, progression, passion, intellect, slavery, deceitful, competitive, restless, unconventional. The 5 is open on both sides it touches the material and has an alter to the spiritual on top. It symbolises Human existence.

6 Responsibility, protection, caring, healing, beauty, harmony, balance, meddling, jealousy, guilt, unfaithful, bitter, opinionated. The 6 is the first perfect number and symbolises Beauty or Ugliness in all their forms.

7 Analysis, understanding, awareness, knowledge, studious, meditative, sage, distrustful, anti-social, impersonal, proud. The 7 is rooted in the material with an alter to the Spiritual at the top. It symbolises Spiritual connection.

8 Influential, powerful, ambitious, authoritative, strong, success, visionary, ruthless, greedy, controlling,

belligerent, manipulative. The 8 is formed two joined circles, above and below. It symbolises the bridge between the material and the spiritual and Infinity.

9 Masterful, competent, determined, honest, efficient, selfless, loving, wise, arrogant, fearful, drifter, emotional, unfocussed. The 9 touches the material but its main body is in the spiritual and it symbolises domination and control.

There are lots (I nearly wrote numerous) books on different types of Numerology. All of them will describe the qualities of the individual numbers as above and when you consider that something as banal as a number, a single digit, could possess attributes that are unique to it, the mind wants to reject the concept.

It's one of the beliefs that's been programmed in. The same sort of belief that dismisses Astrological influences or an Invisible control structure. The fundamental importance and nature of Numbers are another veil.

Numbers don't just have the qualities described above, they can also make geometric shapes – at least 3 and above can. 4 gives the first 3-dimensional shape (a 3-sided pyramid) at and after which, Numbers can become **solids,** and matter can take form!

Everything which we perceive as reality can be described by Numbers. In the Movie, The Matrix they attempt to portray this in numerous scenes, but in particular when the Neo character sees reality as streaming code – himself included.

Were we able to perceive reality as it is, or at least closer to its numerical origins we would see a reality that is visibly changing continuously and dominated by geometric forms. I suspect it is how we first experience things as new-borns. It would explain why Babies are so disoriented for the first few months!

Our minds need to reconcile what we **see** with what we **feel**, **hear, smell, taste** etc. What we **believe** we see is a cleverly constructed collage that's all done automatically and learned long before we can remember, in the earliest months of infancy, so we know for instance what soft **both** looks **and** feels like.

Pythagorean Numerology I've found to be (usually) accurate, but it's clearly not definitive. If it was everyone would have heard of it and use it.

I suspect its practise is allowed precisely because it isn't totally reliable, but can you imagine what it would be like if you could accurately do so? I'll come back to this, but before I do, I just want to mention Sacred Geometry.

Geometry is concerned with properties of space such as the distance, shape, size, and relative position of figures. Sacred Geometry is the geometric properties of Life, The Universe and Everything. It has been used to plan and execute a lot of buildings from the Pyramids of Giza to the layout of Washington D.C. and the Vatican.

https://www.youtube.com/user/secretsinplainsight I found to be a good place to look at the application of Sacred

Geometry in city planning and construction in a very matter of fact way non conspiratorial way.

The layout and design of many cities obey Sacred Geometry and are **not** coincidences. The builders behind these architectural works knew **exactly** what they were doing **and** why. They believed by applying the principles of Sacred Geometry the buildings and their Architects would have power over future events.

It is not for me to argue one way or the other, except to acknowledge that whoever oversees the World has done so successfully for a long time....

I have spent a lot of time researching the methods and activities of the Invisible controllers and the methods they use to communicate with Symbolism.

I've noticed that the content and timing of widely reported events, whether it's News, Sport Results even Natural disasters **always** have numerological significance. Don't take my word for it, do your own research and you'll discover this yourself.

This is so significant, so disturbing, that it took quite a while to process. My Ego did not want to accept this because of the implications. It means **everything** is foretold, including you reading this!

It also means someone, or something has this foreknowledge, while I don't.

If the future within a Holographic reality is not completely fixed, it's reasonable to conclude that some parts e.g. Those events that are felt and experienced by large groups of Humans **are**.

It also means that whatever I thought I was, I am reducible to numbers - an **Algorithm** - and that is a lot to process. I did not want to accept this as even a possibility! A coherent collection of Energy that is self-aware with the ability to observe and record. It has no mass but is arranged in such a way that it can learn and expand. A Child of God, a spark of the Creator.

Wow! On this particular occasion its portal into reality has selected this Human being / physical body to be its avatar, alongside billions of others each having a unique but shared experience. It's possible.

Pythagorean Numerology associates each letter of the alphabet with a number, plus everyone's date of birth is made up of numbers. By analysing the numbers derived from a person's full birth name and their date of birth, it describes their personality, characteristics, and the path their Life is going to follow.

It's like a unique barcode assigned to all Humans who incarnate on Earth.

Another layer of complexity is created by the ancestral DNA where physical and behavioural characteristics are expressed through the physical body. DNA is made up of nucleic acids, four on each strand, each one has a letter – A,C,G or T.

Overlay this with the influence of Astrological bodies and another layer of complexity is added. No two Humans can ever be exactly the same, even if they're algorithms running on autopilot, **everyone** is unique **and** special.

The experiences we have as individuals are unique to us. It is impossible to accurately imagine what it is like to be someone else, how they feel, how they think, how they perceive the World. All are unique.

Astrology is an extremely complex subject.

I've observed the effects of the Sun and Moon. They govern the tides, and the energy involved in moving the Oceans as they do is significant. The Human body is over 70% water, so whether I am conscious of it or not, I too am influenced by the Sun and Moon.

The same can be said for all the other Astrological bodies. They have an influence. It might be subtle, but it's there. Personally, I've notice that the Moon affects me noticeably, particularly when its full.

I consulted an experienced Astrologer towards the end of 2021. It was interesting. Before sharing my report with me, he tried to explain that it would not be a forecast of events, but rather the weather I would experience.

It would help me anticipate whether life was going to be plain sailing or require additional effort. I remembered it, so I could pass it on here (probably). It was a good explanation.

He also urged me not to feel bound by anything in the report. Foreknowledge gives an opportunity to demonstrate free-will and transcend whatever might otherwise have unfolded. I'm not totally convinced on that, but maybe....

As far as I can tell, neither Numerology or Astrology predict or anticipate an Awakening. **If** this is true, an Awakening **might** change's the subject's future. They become self-aware, aware that they are now more than the sum of their parts and can transcend their program.

The extent to which this impacts the collective experience is a curious question. Jung wrote about a collective subconscious and how concepts can arise simultaneously across the Planet.

Perhaps when a certain number or people start Awakening, something will be triggered en masse, but I'm not holding my breath!

Coincidentally in the Christopher Nolan Movie, Tenet, the plot revolves around the possession of an algorithm that gives its possessor the ability to reverse time.

In the film it's depicted as some sort of cyber punk machine assembled from **9** components. The protagonist succeeds in keeping the algorithm from the wrong hands, thereby avoiding the end of the World. I wonder which World he was saving. My perception was that it was the status quo World.

If an algorithm already exists that governs the past and the future, how would it respond if many Humans became self-aware? When you read about Artificial Intelligence in the News, it is also being used by the minions of the Invisible controllers as a message between them. Symbolically AI represents Humanity.

From a certain perspective the intelligence represented by Humanity **is** Artificial due to the way it's hypnotised and conditioned. If the AI singularity represents a Great Awakening, what does that actually mean? What will Humanity be Aware of that was formerly hidden?

If it's **only** the first veil of deception i.e. our rulers are Satan worshipping pedo's who have been blackmailed into fronting a global criminal syndicate, then I don't see a calm outcome, but who knows. Que sera, sera.

Numbers can be so utterly beautiful and awe inspiring. Just look at these:

1 x 8 + 1 = 9

12 X 8 + 2 = 98

123 X 8 + 3 = 987

1234 X 8 + 4 = 9876

12345 X 8 + 5 = 98765

123456 X 8 + 6 = 987654

1234567 X 8 + 7 = 9876543

12345678 X 8 + 8 = 98765433

123456789 X 8 + 9 = 987654321

I have no idea what the significance of this patten might be, it's just so beautiful, unexpected, and elegant I thought I'd put it in. I'm sure someone will tell me. The Fibonacci sequence (1,1,2,3,5,8,11 etc.) is definitely significant, as it dominates the form of the Natural World from flower petals to Galaxies.

Fractals are another curiosity that abound in the Natural World. Solar systems are like Galaxies. The forms adopted by Trees are like Rivers or nervous systems. The mirroring of form is not a coincidence **and** is important.

If everything runs on Numbers, then to what end? Why does God use them to create all the staggering diversity and wonder of reality. The logical conclusion is that God plays **Games** or, if you prefer, conducts experiments.

'All the World's a stage'.

This is probably one of the **deepest** hidden Truths my inquiry led me to. Like all things it's hidden in plain sight. The following hypothesis is the most logical and coherent that I've found.

Tropes referencing the **Game of life** or **Life is just a Game** are ones that everyone recognises but are not necessarily understood. We are conditioned to dismiss them as whimsy, nothing more, but when you consider the purpose of existence logically, it becomes undeniably literal. This does **not** mean that our incarnations are unimportant or simply entertainment for our immortal Souls.

The Universe is supposedly 14.8 billion years old. It's also infinite. This is a contradiction, but I'll use it as the basis of an argument by saying it's wrong by eternity.

Eternity gives ample scope for the evolution, development, and deployment of Games. So realistic they are indistinguishable from our known reality, because one of them **is** our known reality. Complete with shit, boredom, and miserable weather from time to time.

Another of the big hidden truths is that of our true nature – immortal souls. We are not 'Earthlings'. There are more galaxies, stars, and planets harbouring Life than can be counted and yet we believe we're all Alone on this third rock from the Sun. Lol.

Physicists agree there are other Dimensions beyond this one. In those dimensions it's unlikely they have money. Money is a concept that just doesn't work long term. Even on Earth, its origins are relatively recent – at most a few thousand years.

The Hermetic principle of cause and effect explains that something happens because of something else. In an exchange of goods or services there is a concept of quid pro quo – something for something.

Within this hypothesis, higher Life forms trade in (among other things) Games.

On Earth we do not realise we're playing a Game. It's designed that way and it's the foundation stone of the deception. **Not** knowing **who** you are and **why** you are here gives an authenticity to our experiences that cannot be replicated any other way.

Within our existing system, we are conditioned to believe we are simply mortal and the concept that everything is an elaborate Game being played by our Immortal Souls is **difficult** to even consider. I struggled with it.

When you assume this position though, and you look beyond **this** iteration of the Game, you can see that we could (at an ever-higher level) be playing a Game where we are playing this Game as part of **that** Game etc. If the film Inception comes to mind, don't be surprised, it came to mine.

Many of us, me included, have been drawn to playing Video Games. The development of Virtual Reality as a form of entertainment is a coincidence, among too many to count, that indicate we are heading into a future where totally immersive and realistic game play will be realised.

What if we're already there and have been for Eternity?

The process of selecting and creating our Avatars for game play, mimics the function played by our higher selves in planning our incarnation. Having the **same** life over again, or being able to respawn, is a difference from the game we play as human forms, but otherwise the similarities are very striking.

Knowing that you are playing a Game, fundamentally changes the nature of the experience. It creates an emotional detachment. **Understanding** that you are playing a Game does not mean you treat it as something flippant.

You can move from the stage to the audience then back to the stage again. You can observe cause and effect, become sensitive to rhythm, understand polarity and begin to recognise them as they play out around and within you.

The Game is the **only** mechanism that God has to create all the diversity we recognise. Everything is part of God. Nothing can be made, nothing destroyed, all that can be done is to **play**.

It was difficult for me to **understand** the implications of being immortal, but by logical deduction it means:

1. The Human form has been engineered to accept an animating force - spirit.

2. Without Spirit it cannot properly function.

3. All Life on the Planet has been engineered as well.

4. My Higher self is **not** Human – **nor is anyone else's**.

5. Extra Terrestrials are already here and have been for thousands, perhaps millions of years or longer.

6. Everyone has a role to play, every role is different **and** important.

Who we are is a spiritual being. **What** we are is a physical form that owes its design to entities beyond our limited comprehension. **Why** we are here is revealed through the course of our Lives, but the primary purpose is to **learn**.

These conclusions took a lot of assimilating. It's taken over two years for me to accept them as probable, primarily because it took a big effort to admit I was a fraud.

I was so convincing at pretending to be a fifty something Human male, that I convinced myself as well. Just as I convinced myself when I was 7 or 32 or any of the other archetypes I've acted out.

I did this to create a sense of identity. That sense of identity was the version of my ego I projected. It came into existence before I could remember, and it resembled (in my mind) a huge pile of books. Each book containing an iteration of the ego. Youngest at the bottom, current at the top.

Each was slightly different from the preceding one. When a Spiritual teacher talks about dissolving the ego, I've taken that to mean, you gently shove this huge pile of books to one side and find out what they've been concealing.

It doesn't mean destroying the Ego, it means going **back** to who you really are, or originally were. Perhaps that is why some of those who complete their journey of enlightenment are described as childlike who take nothing seriously afterward.

This would seem to be a logical consequence of pushing to one side all the years of conditioning and finding your core ego, which is playing a Game.

The Higher Self should have a chapter on its own, but **my** Higher Self has incarnated here to, among other things, learn humility, so its insights are revealed here at the hands of an unimportant nobody.

The Higher Self or Soul is nonphysical. It is a coherent energy system, and completely self-sustaining. Its intellectual capacity is unlimited, but its capabilities are limited to its **known** experience.

For instance, unless it experiences mortal Human existence, it doesn't understand air, fire, water, earth, food, or rest, or how they interact.

It can manifest its appearance to others in any form it wishes. It can look Human if it wishes to, as it exists outside of Time and Space, but I imagine it as being like a jelly fish or a floating cloud with fine filaments trailing beneath it.

Within the cloud are collected all the Lives lived both here and elsewhere. The filaments are the energetic link between the Higher Self and its many incarnations. Your Higher Self plays in multi-player mode.

Each incarnation represents an energy investment. The Higher Self invests part of **itself** directly **and** retrieves it on completion of the physical Life. Sometimes this process is seamless, sometimes it isn't, but on collection of **all** its returned parts, the Higher Self can move on to unknown adventures.

The **nature** of **The Game** is experiential. It's not a win or lose type of Game and approaching it as if it is, in my opinion, a mistake. The characters we encounter in **our** Game are all playing their parts, including our own.

This was something that I've been able to reflect on as I've spent time re-evaluating the formative experiences in my life. When I viewed it objectively and allow myself to observe all the characters (including me) as Actors, it changed everything.

The more I did this, with my most **painful** memories, the more I learned. It wasn't easy, I had to forgive so many people for the hurt they'd caused, but as importantly I had to forgive myself for what I'd done as well.

I also held opinions about various celebrities where I had an emotional response towards them. While I knew that I didn't really know anything about who they really are, I still had a like/dislike opinion of them.

This was an important lesson for me. The recognition that I liked – for example – Alec Guiness, because he played Obi-Wan Kenobi and other memorable parts and disliked Hilary Clinton because she blamed voters for being stupid when she lost in 2016 **had been a mistake**.

Both were Actors and I know **nothing** about either of them.

The same truth can be applied to our roles in the Game. Of course, most people would want to play the Good parts - the winners, the righteous, the heroic, the daring, but unless someone plays the Bad parts, there is no Balance.

Those playing the Bad parts are no better or worse than those playing the Good parts. When I applied this view to my formative experiences, I no longer blamed my parents for the horrible stuff I saw them do. I now understood and could forgive. **Everyone** is an Actor and the majority play **both** Good **and** Bad.

My parents lived their entire lives Asleep, although my Mother in particular spent a large proportion of her Life seeking answers through religion without success.

Shortly after my Awakening I shared with her what I'd learned. She patiently listened to what I had to say before smiling at me gently like you would if someone you care about was having a mental breakdown. 'You always have to be different Robert don't you.'

Before incarnating, your higher self enters a contract with the Game overseers. This will dictate the course of your incarnation and is coded into your life path. It's reasonable to conclude a few things:

That you'd agree to be a parent or not.

You'd agree to be Asleep, for some or all the incarnation.

You'd agree that your perception of reality was limited to the 5 physical senses.

You'd agree to suffer, physically and mentally.

You'd agree how long you would live.

You'd agree that Time and Space are real.

You'd agree to forego any memory of who you truly are **and** your contract.

What an Amazing Game!

To Play or not to Play?

I watched a thirty-year-old interview with the Psychonaut Robert Monroe on Youtube. He talked about a meeting he had with an entity in the Astral realm. It was from another system and was here on a cruise. Earth was the last of around **100** stops and the entity shared what he'd been told about Earth in the cruise brochure.

He described Earth Game as a **Loosh** farm. He used the term Loosh rather than Love, because Loosh contains the energy of all the emotional spectrum – positive and negative. We are conditioned to associate 'Love' with only positive connotations, but everything else has polarity so why not Love? I will call it **Love**.

The creators of what we know as our Universe, discovered that Love could be produced in massive quantities by the species occupying Earth. Humans are huge producers. The contribution declines with emotional capacity, so insects and plants don't produce much.

Where does all this generated Love go? It is collected and sent back to whoever created this environment in the first place, where it is used elsewhere. The Love is generated throughout an individual's existence, but there's a massive release when the physical body dies.

Sounds a bit like the Matrix, doesn't it?

There's plenty of stuff on the internet about Earth being a prison Planet, Soul farm whatever but I don't subscribe to those views for one very important reason.

It's a Game! Who am I to object anyway? I supposedly **knew** what Earth was before incarnating here. The immortal spiritual aspect of me/I **cannot be imprisoned anywhere.**

At one level it appears to be like the Stanford Experiment. Guards and inmates, and just like the experiment all of us are really students pretending to be a Guard or an inmate, but **forgetting who we truly are**.

There are now reportedly over 8 Billion of us on the Planet.

Hans Rosling, the late statistician, estimated that Human population would peak at 11 Billion around 2100 and then go into decline, but it could peak sooner e.g. 2050. In the developed World, population has already peaked and is declining, most of the growth is going to be in Africa, unless something unexpected happens.

It would seem logical that this could be indicating part of the Game cycle, but who knows? My observations suggest that there is no great existential threat to Humanity. The Invisible controllers want the majority of Humanity alive but scared of Death.

According to the writings of Monroe, Earth's players are divided between those that incarnate **sequentially** and those that incarnate **simultaneously**.

Sequential incarnations are easier to comprehend where it's logical that each incarnation can build on the lessons learned

/ unlearned from the most recent life lived. That's where the beliefs about Karma reside.

Some sequentials' are **always** able to recover their memories of previous lives. Some are born into the **same family's** lifetime after lifetime.

Most sequentials' progress slowly. Two steps forward one step back or vice versa. It takes a **lot** of incarnations to learn, graduate and move on.

Simultaneous incarnations are exactly what they seem. The same Soul incarnates simultaneously into hundreds of Biological Entities (Humans) across **all** of History in **all** ethnicities, genders, orientation etc. from a place that is **outside** our Space Time continuum.

This is difficult to get, but in fiction - C.S. Lewis's The Lion the Witch and the Wardrobe the children enter another World (Narnia) and on their return they discover that Years in Narnia = Hours on Earth. Different dimension, different time behaviour.

It can be hypothesised that Years on Earth = Hours in the Higher Dimensions, where our Souls reside (if they measure their time in a similar way to here). In addition, their capacity to play simultaneously may be beyond my limited imagination, but not their capabilities.

The concept of Sequential vs Simultaneous incarnations is interesting and possible. It could be described it as a polarity choice made by immortal Souls where simultaneous =

diversity and sequential = conformity, perhaps both are needed to maintain balance.

Applying the Law of Correspondence - there will be similarities between dimensions – As Above, So Below. Therefore, other Dimensions **correspond** with this one. There is Good and Bad. Things are partly true and partly false. There are differences within polarities.

A passing visitor from a higher dimension might enjoy playing just a single round (incarnation) of The Earth Game.

Before the incarnation, it learns that it's called 'Titanic'.

In advance it agrees with the Game overseers exactly when it is going to be born and die, its name, gender, personality etc. and a whole Lifetime of interactions with other people. Once set, its Avatar is created – wiped of all memories – and is born on Earth.

At the age of 46 it boards the Titanic on its maiden voyage. By this time, it's a professional Musician and it's a working trip.

Can you guess how it ends!

After a lung full of Atlantic seawater, the mortal remains sink into the abyss, while the non – physical self, returns to where it originally came from.

For the whole of the incarnation beginning to end it was ignorant of its true identity. It believed **it was** the physical body it was occupying. All the interactions it experienced up until the body died were planned so that eventually it would board the ship.

I found this difficult to accept this as even a possibility. I spent 56 years living a Life where I believed that **I** made decisions, where my thoughts were mine and only my mine. My emotional experiences were authentic. I **felt** Joy, Anger, Boredom and all the rest of the emotional spectrum, but I'm also prepared to consider that they were planned as well.

Back to the Titanic though. What if the Musician 'woke up' before boarding the ship? They might realise they were not who they originally thought they were.

Could they **see** through the veil and be aware that they were an Actor on the stage of the World. An Avatar of something else.

If they did Awaken it would appear to be **another layer** of the experience. They might **feel** they were in control; however, they would still board the Titanic.

Awakening reveals the absurdity of how we live our lives, but **it doesn't reveal the Future** (not to me anyway). In this respect the Awakening Avatar is still subjected to deception as its Higher Self **already knows how the story should play out.**

This strongly suggests that free will is an **illusion**, but there is another explanation. **Free will** is synonymous with the Principles of **Correspondence** and **Cause and Effect.**

There is a correspondence between your higher self and the overseers of the Game, a quid pro quo. There must be an incentive for the overseers, otherwise why would they create this amazing reality for us.

I have adopted the hypothesis that the capacity of an Immortal Soul to **do** anything is limited to its abilities and to acquire those abilities it needs to acquire **knowledge**. Earth is, among other things, a **school** and a **quarantined environment**.

This is where we **learn** about **cause and effect** and **correspondence** without blowing up the rest of creation by accident! We are in a spiritual kindergarten. Our purpose here is not to grow older, but to **grow up!**

The suffering we experience as well as the joy is a **price** of playing the Game. So, in that context it is indeed a Love Farm. If you subscribe to Karmic law, **we** farm and consume Animals and Plants from the Planet, **we are conditioned to believe that we are at the top of the food chain, but it appears we're not.**

The reward for our emotional output being consumed is the **knowledge** acquired through our **direct personal experiences** and knowledge is a valuable commodity to anything that wants to grow and evolve intellectually.

The Future is the undiscovered country, but my intuition is that at some level it is as fixed and solid as the past. If you can accept the concept of fatalism, it has a polarity.

At one extreme the emotion we associate with the inevitability of unfolding events could be despair, pessimism, or apathy. At the other there's excitement and anticipation. Somewhere near the middle is curious observation.

It's a Game. I have now invested nearly 59 Earth years in this Game and for 57 of them I had no idea I was playing! If the purpose of it is to learn, I'm looking forward to whatever unfolds.

As stated at the beginning of this section Earth is supposed to be one of at least **100 different Games.** If that's correct, no doubt there are many **millions more**.

It's worth bearing in mind that the Earth Game scenario is based upon (among other sources) **an interstellar cruise brochure**. If it's anything like an Earth cruise brochure it **could** be a bit misleading!

What could they like, the other Games in the brochure?

I imagined incarnating on a different Planet. On this Planet I am in Human form again, there are other options in other Worlds, but I enjoy the sensations associated with being Human, so pick this one.

There is only one ethnicity. There are no individual nation states. There is no religion of any kind. There is no Authority in charge. Money doesn't exist. There are no Wars. Humans live in harmony with each other and their environment. They don't wear clothes and communicate telepathically.

They **know** that they are immortal beings experiencing what it's like to be mortal. They do not Fear death and live on average for 800 years. Every time they incarnate, they carry all the memories from their previous lives to their current one.

That may sound a bit John Lennon, but it's possible. A life as a mortal free of deception and fear.

How long could you imagine doing this before you got bored? How long would it take you to learn all that you wanted to know or experience? How could you speed things up, how could you learn more?

Intriguing, isn't it? Perhaps you'd play a different Game?

To make a clear point my imagined alternate Game is one that is at a very different polarity to the Earth Game amongst many different Games. That said the Game on Earth is obviously towards the Darker polarity.

That doesn't make it either Good or Bad, just different.

Earth Game maybe Dark, but it exists on two distinct levels:

Macro Game – This is the background Drama – The Collective Experience

Micro Game – Your Drama – The Personal Lived Experience

The Micro exists **within** the Macro. It doesn't necessarily mean that they are the same as each other, but they do overlap.

All anyone can expect to influence is the Micro i.e. **Me**. Wasting time and energy on influencing the Macro was one of the lessons I had to learn. I have faith that whatever the Game has in store for me will unfold exactly as it's supposed to.

By recognising and accepting that I and I alone am solely responsible for everything that has and will happen, it has allowed me to release much of the emotional burden I didn't even know was there.

I am solely responsible because **I agreed** to be here to experience **this** life. You may wonder why anything would want to experience Earth. You've got eternity and done everything else, so why not? As it is, I still think Earth is wonderful, although it clearly does have its Dark side.

Perhaps that what makes Light side so glorious, but they are co-dependant. You can't have one **without** the other.

"Oh, what a tangled web we weave, when first we practice to deceive!"

This would be incomplete if I made no reference to how the World operates at the collective level. **Like everything else, you should do your own research and come to your own conclusions.**

In his most acclaimed work - The Wealth of Nations, Adam Smith introduced the concept of the Invisible hand that governed economic outcomes. It asserts that Human beings **always** act in their own self-interest.

Self-interest is **not** the same as selfish.

And there it is, in plain sight. The **Key** that allows a tiny fraction of 1% of the population to herd the rest of us, asleep to the fact that we're being Psyop'd into **believing** whatever our self-interest **is**.

It doesn't matter whether your self-interest is to make loads of money or devote yourself to caring for others or the Planet. If you're Asleep you're going to act based upon your **beliefs** and that makes everyone predictable.

The controllers have decided that they will be invisible. They consider Humanity as Sheep to be herded. It's a strategy that's worked well for them for thousands of years, however despite this, **they still leave tracks.**

It doesn't take much imagination to realise that Royalty, Politicians, Lawyers, Civil Servants, Bankers, Intelligence agencies, Reporters, Publishers, Writers, Actors, Musicians, Police, Educators, Military, Doctors, Other Influencers, in short anyone in a position to either influence people and or events, is a Shepherd or a Sheep Dog.

They are the face of the System that we all recognise. They maintain the System as they are integral to it. If the System collapsed, they would have no function. The herd would be scattered to the four winds and getting it back would take a lot of resources.

I have in the past been a government employee and worked in Banking, but at no point did I consider myself as a Sheep Dog and, I have no doubt that most people working in the sectors above would feel the same.

The individuals at the very top of these sectors know **exactly** what their role is and will follow their orders from the controllers without question. In turn they control all the other Shepherds beneath them and on to the Sheep dogs.

Blackmail is the primary mechanism by which the upper-level Shepherds loyalty is secured. **Most** of these individuals **volunteer** to be blackmailed as they **already understand** how the system works and if you aspire to be a famous Actor or Politician, you'll need to already come from one of the approved (Shepherd) bloodlines (unless you're VERY talented) **and** prepared to pay the price.

You may feel that the nature of this blackmail, including murder and paedophilia is too much to ignore, but if you want to penetrate the veil it's helpful to put it to one side. Not to ignore it but to look **beyond** it.

I've hypothesised that the revelation of such crimes is being used to trap Awakening individuals. Some, understandably, become champions of the oppressed and do everything they can to publicise the horrors and call for justice. They cannot see beyond that veil.

I've noticed how Sheep Dogs herd. They do **not** directly attack the Sheep. They use **psychology** to influence the Sheep's behaviour. They may threaten, coerce, distract, confuse, or drive them, but they don't directly attack.

In many respects, they are no different and no freer than the Sheep. Just a different class of slave, which was an important observation for me, as it applies equally to Humanities Shepherds and Sheep Dogs.

I suspect most of the Shepherds do not realise this and are NPC's, even the upper-level ones. Some of the Shepherds may also be Awakening and I can imagine it's far more challenging for **them** as opposed to a Handyman!

Just as there is a hierarchy with the Herd, so there is with the Shepherds. The Shepherds at the top of the chain, those who **actually know** what they are doing amount to much less than **1%** of the population.

The most senior Shepherds have their own Belief system, which involves worshipping the Invisible controllers, who are not even on the Planet. They are of the belief that they are very different to the Herd – Special – anointed by God in their Divine roles.

Except it's a deception. They are not anointed by God, but A God and you can probably guess which one. Whatever anyone calls him, he is like everything else – part of the consciousness that is Everything, but not The All.

Sacrifice is a **big** part of their religion, not just us, but **themselves**. They willingly go along with it, primarily because it works, **and are born into it**.

I'm not going to start a list of high-profile Shepherds here, it isn't necessary. You can do your own research, but if there are any celebrities, artists, scientists, politicians etc. who you **believe** you like, prepare to be **very** disappointed.

The top Shepherds have access to technology that is so far beyond our current understanding that it is the stuff of Science Fiction. They can control the Weather, trigger Earthquakes and Volcanic eruptions.

Sobering stuff for anyone who aspires to putting on the Armour of God intent on overthrowing the system but it's worth noting that it's **their** Game at the collective level, and **we knew** what we were incarnating into **before** we got here.

To achieve and maintain control, the Shepherds employ various techniques, with the primary strategy of **Divide and Rule**.

It is the way of keeping yourself in a position of power by causing disagreements among other people so that they are unable to oppose you. To maintain power, the ruler supports **all** sides.

This is impossible for those who are Asleep to understand. As soon as you make a judgement over something being Good or Bad, Right or Wrong, you become controllable.

They employ Good Guy, Bad Guy to persuade you to choose a polarity. Trump is an excellent example of a polarizing character. We are encouraged to either Love or Loathe him. **It doesn't matter which you choose, as long as you make a choice.**

Clever, isn't it? It works because we are predictable. We are bred for purpose and educated to make binary decisions. This is right or that is wrong - and we fall into their web of beliefs, opinions, biases and lies. So simple, but so effective.

It is done by stimulating us into an emotional response, usually via TV or social media. Emotions are tied to beliefs, and beliefs are both malleable (they can be influenced) and exploitable by those who know how to do it.

There was a time when I **believed** without reservation in Western medicine, Democracy, History, the News, and Science. I also held a Saviour belief where we believe that there could be, should be, someone who can lead us. And look at what we get. Lol.

The system is primed to attack anyone or anything that attacks it. Any attempt to persuade someone to Awaken will be dealt swiftly by the conditioning. The subject will label you as psychotic, **I would have done so**. The harder you press your case, the more psychotic you will appear.

Should you attempt to reach a mass audience it's unlikely you'd succeed – they own the internet. If you do manage to break through, you'll be met with an avalanche of shit, or worse.

Attacking the system is a likely bad idea. If you believe that's what you came here to do, just ask yourself if that's true, or the idea of it is filling some sort of emotional need. If it's the latter, you've been played. Speaking as someone who has fallen for it many many times, I have been played **all** my Life.

"The road to Hell is paved with good intentions."

I spent a couple of decades selling stuff – mainly intangibles like money (loans) and insurance – stuff you can't see. I got pretty good at it too. I enjoyed it, or at least the buzz from closing a sale.

I learned how it worked, I sought to understand, but I never fully did. It was only recently that I realised I'd been practising Magic.

Selling is both a Science and an Art and for some reason I never consciously applied it on family. I resolved to leave my sales archetype at the office and be authentic at home. It wasn't so clear in my mind at the time, but with hindsight it's what I did and I'm glad I did so.

My first experience of understanding Sales was when I was taught something called 'Guided discovery'. It was a strategy where a customer would learn (discover) that they had a pressing need to buy a product they'd never thought of buying before.

Here's an example:

A customer has just decided to buy a car on finance and the payments are about £ 450 / month.

"Mr Customer. You've made a great decision to lease this beautiful car. I was wondering though, how would your standard of living be affected if you had to take time off work sick, or you unexpectedly lost your job?"

"Would it go up or **down**?"

"Errrrrr down"

"How would you feel if **someone else paid your lease** if that happened?"

"Errrrr, I'd like that"

The customer now finds themselves agreeing that they would like Payment Protection Insurance and the rest is a multi-Billion-pound miss selling scandal.

When you understand how these sales processes are structured, you see them mirrored in how we're manipulated into acting in our own self-interest.

"Mr Citizen. You're a member of this society, but how would it be affected with a serious novel respiratory illness sweeping through it?

Would it get better or worse?

"Errrrr worse"

"How would you feel if you were able to make a difference and help society while protecting yourself and others?"

Enough said.

When I was taught these techniques, I did not appreciate just how pervasive and transferable they were and while I appreciated, they were exploiting psychology, I did not consider them Magic.

When I observed billions of Human beings offering their shoulders to be injected with a substance with unknown consequences, it forced me to re-assess what Magic actually looked like, because this was it.

Was it the same Magic that persuaded millions to go to War?

I'm sure it was, but with hindsight, it's surprising it took me so long for the penny to drop. My father had been in the RAF in WW2 and its legacy had been a formative aspect of my upbringing and therefore conditioning.

Convincing the majority to **believe** in a lie is an incredibly powerful form of Magic and would appear to form the foundation of this civilisation. Money is another example – Fiat (as in Fiat Money) is Latin for By Decree or So Be It.

Money has a value because **everyone agrees** that it does. Fiat money is not backed by anything other than the word of a corrupt system, however it **does** work, because the majority **believe** it does.

Until they get into a mess with inflation, which they usually get out of by inventing a new type of money, which is scarcer than its predecessor and the cycle can then repeat.

My conclusion comes from the observation that no system of recorded governance has ever delivered long term stability and I can see no reason why the time period we live within is going to buck the trend.

Quite the opposite.

In early 2008 I visited San Francisco on business. It was at a conference that I learned about something – the speaker called - The Law of Reciprocity. He explained that Humans are hard wired into it.

For example, if you do something nice or helpful to a friend or neighbour, they will (usually) feel obliged to reciprocate and vice versa. This is also true with complete strangers.

This was / is a vulnerability that can and is exploited. It is something that is just such a natural behaviour to us as Humans, that we don't see it as one. However, for those who want to influence others, it is the Achilles heel of Human beings – they enter through our Soul.

If a stranger approached and gave you a Flower, when you were just having a walk, I suspect it would raise a warm smile and maybe some conversation. If another stranger approached and slapped your face, you'd probably feel like slapping them back.

What I only recently came to understand is that this Law applies universally i.e. an act of selfless generosity is always reciprocated, as are any other acts. Even when the only observer of them is the actor.

In virtually all religious and spiritual teachings, the core message is one of reciprocation. Do unto others as you would have them do unto you. It is a curious coincidence.

While I think it can be an endearing instinct, when demonstrated positively, it can be an awful one when negative **and** it can be exploited.

In the unlikely event that a fleet of interstellar craft appear, who declare that they are here to save us from destruction and to share their technology so we can become a space faring species, I have only one comment.

Beware of Strangers bearing Gifts. Lol

'Fool me once, shame on you. Fool me twice, shame on me'.

The principle of Rhythm explains that everything goes in cycles, it rhymes. A plant emerges from a seed, it goes through a period of growth, it matures and ripens, it withers and returns to the soil. Until another emerges from a seed and the rhythm repeats.

Nothing grows in reverse.

Civilisations go through the same process and ours is no different. There is a flow to events and it's consistently worsening. The last three + years has been strange to say the least. The common thread is usually **Fear:**

Fear of a Virus and Vaccines, Migrants, Police, Government, Poverty, Left and Right, Nuclear War, Economic collapse, Death.

It could be a much longer list, but you get the point. When you strip away all the 'details' about anything in the 'News' **Fear** is normally at the **Heart** of the story. It's not a coincidence.

Every now and again there'll be someone's story of **Despair,** to break the monotony.

Returning to the theme of rhythm, 1960 heralded a new era, it was 63 years ago (which is 7 x 9 years) so the principle of rhythm indicates there **may** be similarities with then. 1897 was another 63 years before. It had echoes of 1960. Not the same, but similar.

Go back another 126 years and you arrive in 1771. The 1770's was a decade of invention, revolution, and upheaval, which produced great changes. 63 years later at around 1834 was yet another time of upheaval and revolution.

The 60's descended into the horrors of the Cuban missile crisis, JFK, Vietnam etc. but it also marked the beginning of the sexual revolution and saw an explosion in cultural and artistic endeavours.

In the intervening years, apart from computing and communication, all our other technologies have remained almost static.

Improvements have been marginal to cars and aircraft etc. Cities have grown, the farmland industrialised. Health outcomes in the West are now worse than the 60's. We live longer only to suffer longer. The divisions within our societies are different divisions than they were, but societies still have divisions.

Being objective, it is only a matter of when not if this civilisation will collapse, or at least the system that governs it. Questions like can it be fixed? Or What can stop it? Are the wrong questions.

A collapse of the system is as certain as the fact that a beautiful flower will wither and die. Why should anyone be frightened of a natural process? We can do nothing but

watch the petals curl and fall. Out of its demise, new shoots emerge. It does it all by itself.

The current flow appears to be towards a global totalitarian government. The strategy being to destroy public confidence in established systems of governance so that a One World Government is the only solution.

The rationale that the elites believe is that it is the **only way** to avoid a catastrophic collapse. This **appears** to be mostly True, however by scrutinising this subject, appearances can change. This is a Game.

Why would the invisible controllers feel the need to have a World Government in the light, when they **already are** in the shadows? The only logical explanation is that it's **yet another deception**.

The evidence of their plan is overwhelming and well documented. Why would you make it so easy for your plan to be understood by those who could foil it? Presumably, because that's exactly what will happen.

Are we not seeing Good Guy / Bad Guy being played on an epic scale? The Bad Guys (World Banks, WEF, Bill Gates, UN, WHO etc.) are doing their best via corrupted politicians to destroy global prosperity.

The Bad Guys appear to be inept, arrogant, and suicidal. The Good Guys are **everyone else**. Trump, Putin and Xi Jin Ping could easily be recorded in history as Good Guys. Ironic as they are **all** on the same side!

This may seem unlikely, but while even recent History is subject to dispute, there are some facts tied to events that are difficult to argue against. In World War 1, tens of millions died in what turned out to be a pointless war. In World War 2, many more millions were **sacrificed** to the same cause.

As a baby boomer I was brought up on the tales of daring do in WW2 and as I grew to be a young man, I felt a yearning to be able to do my patriotic duty like my father before me.

What **insanity** this was. Relatively few people in authority on either side have ever been held accountable for the senseless slaughter of either conflict. It's embedded into our **cult**ure. Our willingness to sacrifice ourselves, and ignore the forces compelling us to do so, is demonstrably true.

I never understood how the German people were fooled into following Hitler and how they continued to support him (apparently) until the very end. The 2020 Pandemic answered my question. I would have probably been an early adopter Nazi, who would have turned away in 1936. Lol

The important observation from all these examples is that a large chunk of the Herd is compliant. They will do as they are told by the authorities and encourage others to do so as well, for as long as they **believe** in the system.

Every single person on the Planet is being tested and most are unlikely to pass. I'm not being arrogant or pessimistic about this, but realistic. It's a Game. No-one really dies and it's not supposed to be easy.

The rule I follow is simple. It's better to be Alone walking in the **right** direction than with a crowd of people going the wrong way. **I** don't have to **do** anything **I** don't want to do. The same applies to everyone. **Be strong**. **Trust your instincts**.

By and large, when there is some sort of cull, you are required to sacrifice yourself – **of your own free will**.

The overarching theme of this period appears to be the transition of Humanity on Earth from the Age of Pisces (Believing) into the Age of Aquarius (Knowing). I think it's reasonable that the power of belief will eventually make way to the power of knowing.

But belief appears to be going out with a bang, hence a time of Revelation and Apocalypse - Unknowns become knowns and great changes take place. It is a **very** interesting time to be alive on Earth as our beliefs are destroyed.

This is how we explore strange new Worlds and new Civilisations. We do not get on a ship and teleport down to the surface like Star Trek. As immortal beings, time is not a prime consideration, authenticity is more important. **We live here**.

We have incarnated into physical form precisely, so we are here, right now, in the first person, to experience something very special. Intuitively and logically, it can't be stopped so shouldn't be feared. Over 8 billion beings. All here for the same reason.

Whatever that is remains to be seen. The **future** is the most closely guarded secret of secrets. I've reconciled with myself that it has to be this way or there would be no point in playing this amazing Game.

AI could disrupt society so quickly and so fundamentally that its effects will be like a virtual tsunami. It could destroy a lot of white-collar jobs, although it might take a bit longer before it can fit a Bath panel or fix a dripping tap.

The combination of technological, economic, political, military, and social crises peaking simultaneously is a perfect storm for Western civilisation. That said, it's a contrived sequence of events.

The motto of Freemasonry is **Order from Chaos**. Once you begin Awakening, you see things differently – back to front. Chaos is engineered, so Order can be imposed.

When I think back to what I know of taught History, the years immediately **prior** to the most memorable, are the **most** illuminating e.g. 1913, 1928, 1937, are less memorable but during all these years the portents were clear.

At the time of writing, I suspect we are at a similar point, just waiting for the Black Swan to arrive.

A Black Swan event in financial markets is described as something (usually a major crash) that no-one sees coming in advance but is obvious with hindsight. This is clearly untrue (someone not only sees it coming, but engineers its manifestation) but its accepted as true by the majority.

By the time you read this it may have already occurred. That will not make me a prophet. I keep reminding myself that our perceived reality is a perfect deception, so can only speculate as to the eventual direction Humanity is sent in.

From my very limited understanding of what is happening within the ranks of the ruling elite, they are having their very own existential crisis. They expect to be revealed to Humanity and consequently destroyed.

At least that is the Sum of all **their** Fears, according to the drama that is being played out. I have to admit that **if** 99.9% of the population Awaken to the way the World is run, it would be, well, interesting to see what happens with the 0.1%

Will this be their last and greatest sacrifice? i.e. themselves?

Ultimately Humanity will be offered a choice. That is the where Good Guy Bad Guy **always** leads to. Will it be drawn to the future offered by the Bad Guys or the Good Guys? Will Humanity realise there are **no** Good Guys?

According to Monroe, the drama that is Human existence on Earth has another 1300 years ahead of it, but this point in the story, this time, is an important one. Certainly, worth being here to experience.

Without any beliefs I can't point to any particular system or organisation that appears to be superior to any other system. Perhaps Humanity is being led to an overtly totalitarian system, but as its already a covertly run system, it seems academic.

In order to observe how the controllers minions communicate with each other, I needed to be able to, if not understand at least appreciate symbolism and how it's used to do this.

"One man's meat is another man's treasure"

I've found this a fascinating but difficult subject. Within the layers of control there is a need for the 1% at the top to communicate secretly. To do this, they communicate in plain sight using symbolism.

I am **not** expert at this. It requires the same sort of logic that people who do cryptic crosswords use, where the clues are quite abstract, and you are seeking some sort of double meaning. You will find this symbolism in mass media. It could be the News, or a Movie, or in video Games, or in popular Music.

Whatever the vehicle for the message, it will be high-profile. The News! Sport finals or best-selling video Games, top grossing Movies or TV shows are always rich in hidden meanings.

That said even low-profile vehicles are used where the messages are between smaller factions of the Shepherds.

Once you understand the basics you start to recognise the hidden language being employed, much in the same way that you can recognise someone speaking French or German even if you're not fluent. You can identify the language, even if you don't necessarily understand what is being said.

In the hidden World the most important commodity is **information.** It's worth considering why this might be. The logical answer is best explained by an old saying. 'In the Kingdom of the Blind, the One-Eyed Man is King'.

Knowledge is Power

To **them**, symbolically **Water** is information. It is **clear, transparent and flows.** When it becomes **frozen** it no longer flows. The information is **locked**. When it is **muddy** it is no longer clear and transparent.

The most **powerful** information is **Nuclear** and the **fallout** from nuclear incidents can be devastating.

In 1945 the USA dropped two nuclear bombs on Japan. Each one had a nickname. One was called 'Little Boy' the other 'Fat Man'. Of course, these names reflected the size and shape of the weapons, but what could these names have represented symbolically?

What if they were photographs of an actual Little Boy and a Fat Man? Who could the Fat Man have been and what was he doing with a Little Boy? Someone Japanese, someone important. Who had the photographs?

Japan surrendered unconditionally.

Numbers are often incorporated into News stories and here are just a few examples of what these numbers symbolise:

666/66/6 Deep state.

999/99/9 the 9 is the 6 inverted for those who betray the Deep state.

13 A Target / Unlucky

17 (can also be 71) denotes top secret.

23 Flee!

4 as in fore warning.

33 the highest number in Freemasonry (33rd degree) giving awareness that practitioners of the secret arts are involved in something.

55 or 5:5 Clear signal being communicated.

8 DNA

322 or 223 The order of the Skull and Crossbones. Highest level of the Free Mason's secret societies.

201 Jesuit's. They're secretly the highest-ranking Shepherds.

This list is just the tip of a very large Iceberg. The most useful source I've come across is a blog called https://decodingsymbols.wordpress.com which provides insights on this area of communication. There are other sources as well if you look hard enough.

It appears that there is a belief among many that there is an ongoing war for the control of humanity and its nature can be discerned from studying the use of symbolism.

I don't know about you, but I interpret this as a battle between Shepherds for control of the herd, and I don't consider myself livestock anymore even if I am.

"The truth is not always beautiful, nor beautiful words the truth".

Religion is a difficult subject to cover as it's clearly diverse, however that (for me) made it ultimately easier to deal with. How many different religions are there I wonder? I've only been exposed to Christianity as a practitioner, but know something about Islam, Judaism, Hinduism, Sikhism, Gnosticism and others. Each Religion is further subdivided into different denominations.

It's textbook Divide & Rule.

I'll close this chapter here, except to acknowledge that the application of Religion in all its forms as a mechanism of herd control is both perverse and incredibly clever. It could equally be described as magical.

Awakening some more

"To see a World in a Grain of Sand And a Heaven in a Wild Flower, Hold Infinity in the palm of your hand And Eternity in an hour"

Awakening has changed my Life. It's not something I consciously wished for, it just happened. At least that's what I thought at the time.

Like everything else, once you've changed you can't change back.

I don't know how many times a Soul incarnates on Earth. Some say it's 150, others 1500.

Whatever the number it is, it's more than anyone can reasonably comprehend.

There may be different reasons for Awakening:

1. It creates a wholly different experience. According to several sources, Awakening indicates a final or near final incarnation on Earth. Perhaps a chance to peer behind the curtain now the show is almost over.

2. You have a Mission to complete.

Patience was the first thing I had to learn. I knew something was happening to me, and wanted whatever it was to conclude as soon as possible. It took about 9 months before the initial hysteria subsided.

Meditation proved to be difficult until I stopped trying and focussed on being relaxed, however whatever my Mission was / is would not come to me.

I began to notice, and still do, repeating number sequences, usually when checking the time i.e. 3.33, 12.21 etc. As far as I can tell these sequences don't have a specific meaning but are simply signals to remind you that reality is more than it seems, **and** you are consciously aware of it. They occur too often to be coincidences.

2021 came and went. I was Awakening but still could not find a new direction to take my life in. I was much calmer by the end of the year. Even though I still didn't have a coherent hypothesis to explain what I was experiencing, the seeds were there.

2022 was dominated by my mother's death. She was 92 and had Heart failure. She died in October but spent periods in and out of Hospital for around a year before she eventually died.

Despite all my shadow work and mindfulness, I still found it an emotionally stressful time. However, I learned so much that I now understand why it unfolded as it did for me.

Earlier in the year, partly because I thought it might help me Astral Project but also in recognition that many people had reported receiving insights by doing so, I decided that I'd take a psychedelic trip. I bought a kit and grew my own mushrooms.

It was towards the end of September that I had grown enough to take the plunge. It was a Thursday. Mum was out of Hospital and had helpers going in. Lesley was going out for the day with her sister. There was nothing in the diary and it was a nice day.

Based on my body weight the recommended dose was 3 g for a normal trip and 5 g for a Psychonaut. I went for 4 g, which I cooked into a broth and swallowed down. I opened my journal to record my experience and waited.

Nothing seemed to happen for about 20 minutes and then it began. I had very few preconceptions about what the trip would be like. I wasn't afraid and knew that whatever I experienced it would be just that – an experience.

At the physical level it was like being fairly drunk. My co-ordination was impaired and moving around took concentration and effort. It was the visual effects that were **initially** the most intriguing and bizarre.

Everything was moving. For example, the skin on my hands appeared to be rippling. I had no physical sensations of the movement, it was entirely visual, but it was strange to say the least!

I looked at myself in a mirror. My skin appeared more like that of a reptile, although my form was still identifiably Human. It was intriguing. Colours were exaggerated, appearing almost neon in intensity. The internal doors were all glowing as if illuminated from within.

Then a thought came to me. **It's about Balance**. Just that.

I decided to go outside. It was a warm sunny day and everything in the garden was still in full bloom. I found myself studying a flower. It was stunning. The details were incredibly vivid and yes, it was moving as well.

I looked up to the clear blue sky and saw an arrangement of fine lines across it. It reminded me of a spider's web or a sheet of fine lace. The shapes created by this grid were geometric.

Then I saw the aircraft. There were two of them. Single engine trainers from the local RAF airfield. The lead aircraft had white wings, the following one black. They were dog fighting, or at least pretending to.

As they danced across the sky diving and banking another thought came to me. **Can you see now?** This is what **we** do. We play **Games**. Endlessly chasing we, because that's all there is to do.

Tears filled my eyes. I'd already read Monroe's description of incarnating, but they'd just been words, understood but not known. Now, just like when the first veil dropped, I **knew,** and it was shattering. It's just a Game? Nothing else?

What else did you expect? Flowed another thought.

I felt no mockery or malice behind it. It was like a Loving parent, patiently explaining to an eight-year-old child that had learned the truth about Santa from its mocking friends. 'You believe in Santa, you believe in Santa, ha ha ha'.

Yes, Santa Claus is really **us**. We deceived you because we Love you and wanted you to experience the magic of

Christmas. When you are Grown up and have your own Children, you'll do the same.

There were no apparitions, no blinding flashes of Light. There was just me, looking at my own reflection and seeing that I was still a Child, but one that was finally Growing up.

By the middle of the Afternoon the hallucinations tapered off and I was back to normality, except I'd changed. One of the effects of Psychedelics is that they reset your default mode network (DMN).

Your DMN is basically a collection of internal maps that your consciousness uses to recognise things. It governs your biases and how you interact with others. I'd read about it and thought I understood what this meant, but now I was **knowing** what it meant.

I had let go of **all** my beliefs. I now recognised that I didn't really **believe** anything, and it gave me a new sense of Faith. Whatever was going to happen, there would be some reason for it, and I didn't need to know why or when it was going to happen, just accept it when it did.

I felt fine, but tired. By 9pm I developed a headache and soon after I went to bed and slept soundly. I woke the following morning and sensed that I would need to go again. There was still more to be revealed.

I didn't have much enthusiasm for it, but I undertook two further trips, at the beginning of November and then again at the beginning of December. The second trip revealed to me that I should share my experience with others.

It was a clear understanding, but I had no idea how I would do so. I put it to the back of my mind. My intention for the next trip was that it would be my last. I took 7 g to see if it made any difference. It did, it was more intense.

My head started ringing with the squeal of tinnitus. It got louder and louder until I thought it was going to burst. I lay down on the floor and waited for something to break. When it did and I opened my eyes, Geometric forms dominated my perception.

When I closed my eyes, I could still see the room. Very strange indeed. I opened my eyes again. Everything I saw was vibrating and only took on a solid form when I focussed my attention on it.

I closed my eyes and had a vision of the very first wave form, the beginning of creation. As it expanded it began to interact with itself. More waves appeared. I saw a bright red spark appear from nowhere. It was ricocheting in all directions. The waves continued to expand, and the vision faded.

'They're trying to return to the beginning'. What? 'The Waves - they want to return to where they came from'. This was a really curious thought. The waves want to return to a balanced, neutral state? 'Yes'.

I started to feel nauseous and had to go and throw up. My head was pounding, and I could see what little I'd brought up, floating in the bowl. I was looking down at yet another manifestation of consciousness and grinned ironically.

I made a mental note to remember the unpleasant aspects of these experiences. I had been given enough. I didn't need to do this again. Not for a while anyway.

Afterwards I noticed I was paying attention to natural Life more - Birds, other wildlife and watching plants change day by day as they go through their cycle, untouched by the collective experience. Earth is a truly beautiful place.

I now see my fellow Humans are just like me, each playing their character embodying its archetype, while deep inside, they're another me. I **try** to make no judgements, just observe.

According to various writings some Souls incarnate in groups, taking turns as parents or children, male or female, fleeting or permanent, sibling or spouse. If this is even only partly true, it's entirely possible that my biological family is also my Soul family.

I Love all of them and recognise that, in turn, we are all part of a much larger family who are sharing the same experience. My eldest sister graffitied a message on a wall at our childhood home, which I've never forgotten.

There's no such things as strangers. They're just friends you haven't met.

All Spiritual teachings describe the path to enlightenment as solitary. This is partly True. Only **you** can become enlightened as it's fundamentally an esoteric process, but I've still needed exoteric experience **and** support.

Were it not for the people in my Life, my path would have not been the same. I **know** that I have grown **because** of everyone else, not despite them. This is another of the lessons I've learned.

I'm not detached from the people I Love and watching them suffer is challenging, but they like me they apparently signed up for this. And just like me they are the vehicles of an Immortal Soul – they just don't all know it (yet).

Until they do, I will continue to play my part. A father to my children, a handyman to my customers, a brother to my siblings etc. My insights have equipped me to be a better version of all these roles than I was before, so why not?

When they do awaken, we can all stop pretending to be the physical bodies we occupy and see each other for who we actually are – Spiritual beings sharing a material experience.

Day to day, being as mindful and present as I can be, particularly around others, is all I need to do. I'm not as good at it as I would like to be, which is as good a reason as any to keep trying.

I'm able to watch TV again. It's still full of lies and programming, but I can see it now, and besides I enjoy spotting comms (symbolic messaging) so I have an idea of what might be unfolding in the near future.

I think Awakening might be like the journey of a Salmon back to its spawning ground. You travel by instinct, against the flow of the water. There are many perils and traps waiting to prevent you from reaching your destination.

When and if you reach your final destination (not many Salmon do), your reward for completing the cycle is Death. Despite this, you cannot do anything about it. You are compelled to complete the mission.

"It is better to light a candle than curse the darkness."

Amongst my areas of Inquiry, I came across etymology, the origin and structure of words. I found it particularly illuminating. Here are a couple of examples:

Ignorance and Knowledge.

Ignorance can be described as the **Act of Ignoring**.

Knowledge can be described as steps (**ledges**) of Knowing.

So, what had I spent my Life **ignoring** and, as importantly, **why?**

What I'd been ignoring was paradoxes. The **why** was fairly easy to answer. They are **irreconcilable** (or at least that's what I believed) **and** we are provided with Lies dressed as Truths to resolve them, which form the foundations of our beliefs.

The best examples are the concepts of infinity and eternity. Infinity goes on forever, eternity does the same, except we are conditioned to **believe** that neither of these concepts are true.

We live in a finite Universe that is 14.8 billion years old and on a planet that has existed for about 4.5 billion years. Only a few hundred years ago, it was generally accepted that the Universe was around 6,000 years old.

It's clear that with modern scientific equipment our current understanding is far more accurate than the beliefs adopted by our forebears. Or are they? They still leave unanswered - what existed before, what exists beyond?

By applying critical thinking this is resolvable. For Time to exist it requires a starting point, otherwise it collapses under the weight of its own making. There is no such thing as half of Eternity.

In Eternity there is **no beginning or end**. All that exists is an **infinite Now**.

Therefore, linear Time **is an illusion**. Everything that ever existed or will exist has already happened and is happening everywhere simultaneously. Our minds deal with this paradox very simply. We Ignore it. We **believe** Time is real.

When I read the Hermetic Principles, they were like a candle in the darkness, illuminating the hidden truths that I'd spent my life ignoring. It was only after some **time** had passed that I noticed they were incomplete as they didn't deal with **Time.**

In fact, they **relied** on time without directly referencing it e.g. Cause and Effect relies entirely on the passage of time to produce the proof of principle. You hit the nail with a hammer for it to puncture the timber. It is a linear sequential process.

The same can be applied to all **but** the **principle of mentalism**. In the absence of time, **the other principles are no longer valid**. They **need** time to function.

This doesn’t make them false, but it doesn’t make them true either. What it does mean is that they are not the answer to everything, because they **only** apply within **this** reality.

The construct within which we believe we exist is a Time, Space, **Illusion**, and it’s very very good. It’s just so real that even though I now **know** it’s an illusion, the pizza I ate this evening tasted amazing.

The Love I experience when interacting with others, the aches and pains that greet me when I open my eyes in the morning, the thoughts that flow through and from my open mind are **all** an illusion, but also real.

For a few years my occupation was a trainer. To ‘teach’ means to “show, point out, declare, demonstrate," also "to give instruction, train, assign, direct; warn; persuade,".

What the experience taught me, was I didn’t really teach anyone anything, people only learn. As a teacher, you may be a catalyst for this learning, but you can’t **insert** learning into another. At least not in **this** reality.

The best teachers I’ve met are those that **enable** their students to learn. They are not the most knowledgeable, but those that **inspire** the necessary curiosity and interest for learning to take place.

Curiosity is one of the main things that we are here to develop in this Time, Space, Illusion.

All our incarnations are parts in a comedy drama. Every thought, action, mistake, success, and failure part of the script. We **believe** we are the characters we are playing. We **believe** it's real and therefore it **is real**. FIAT reality.

Only curiosity and persistence can unravel the deception and reveal the purpose of our existence, which is to **learn**. It doesn't matter that our paths are pre-determined, we still learn from the experience, because we don't know what we don't know. It's authentic.

A Soul might intellectually understand fear, loathing, agony, ecstasy and all the rest of the emotional spectrum, but it can't appreciate how they **feel** unless it hitches a ride on a mortal vehicle and has its memory wiped.

With this acquired knowledge it can replicate or at least translate the emotional learning wherever it wants or needs to.

It's a huge pill to swallow, but the implications of a simulated reality resolve many paradoxes.

How is it possible for many different individuals' alive on Earth today to report memories of being the same historically notable someone? You (a Soul) could possibly play whoever you want to be, in whatever period you choose. The Game is permanently running over all time periods and therefore more than one Soul can be the same character. It's a Game.

Can Souls incarnate simultaneously in multiple Human forms during the **same period** on Earth? Why not? It's a Game.

Why do Souls want to experience being evil, selfish, hunger, pain, despairing and all the other negative aspects of Human existence? It's a Game. Without the knowing provided by the negative it's not possible to know the positive.

If everything is scripted, what does this mean for free-will and karma? Within **this** the simultaneous paradigm, karma can only exist within the confines of each incarnation.

Numerology taught me about Karmic debts, which do appear to manifest within individuals' life paths. Why would they be there if they weren't due? Rather than being debts, it's reasonable to categorise them as lessons, handicaps, or both. Rather than being the result of previous mistakes or misdeeds, they are there for illustrative purposes in an overall learning experience.

The most difficult aspect of paradoxes for me is getting an answer I don't like i.e. existing within a fatalistic, pre-determined simulation. It offends every fibre of my physical being, but just because I don't like it, I can longer dismiss it as I would have done before.

'Dismiss' means to send away, presumably so it can then be ignored.

Staying with a fatalistic view and taking the time to really examine it, it's easy to understand why it is so quickly dismissed. Fatalism slips easily and sleekly into defeatism – I mean, why bother with **anything**.

The opposite polarity is **optimism** and the very thing that enables you to choose between the polarities already exists - Time. You cannot see the future, but you **create** the future you experience by **how** you process the present.

At least that's how it feels to me. You cannot make the wrong decision, be late, or early, too fat, too thin, too rich, too poor, or anything else. **You** will always be exactly where you should be doing exactly what **you** should be doing.

If that means being a miserable billionaire or a supremely happy rough sleeper, it's that way because **you** wanted it to be, because **you** want to experience **everything** and **everybody**.

As events have unfolded for me my sense of self has changed significantly. I feel both less and more Human. Less, because I now know that I'm not truly Human. No-one is. More, because this experience is **real** and worthy of attention.

Plato's cave is usually cited as the best allegory for the veils of reality, but the final veil (for me) is that concealing the Soul. What is it, what does it want? The answer to this paradox is not only outside the cave, but outside the physical universe. Can't get much further outside the box!

I've been outside the box so many times now that I don't find this as daunting as it might have been. The answer I've found like all my other insights has the **bitter flavour** of authenticity.

At the Heart of my search is the burning question – **Why!** The answer is gut wrenchingly obvious – **Why not? Someone wanted to see if they could!**

Why did we create Fire? Why did we invent anything – from the Wheel to Atomic bombs or Artificial Intelligence? To see if we **could.** This instinct to push the boundaries and see what lies beyond is what differentiates Humans from all other living species on Earth.

When it was written that God created man in his own image, this was the Truth hidden in plain sight. **God is curious and so are we**. We are all fractals of the creator.

This leads to a curious line of inquiry. What if our Higher Selves have their own paradox – they don't remember where they came from and want to discover their origin?

Our Higher Selves want to know how intelligence will develop in an environment where almost everything is a lie. Pretty sick, but who knows what other experiments are running. This one may be benign by comparison.

Being unconscious of all this does not impact the learning experience. Lessons will be learned (or not) regardless. The Soul will grow and **that** is the objective. The scenario within which each incarnation exists is simply that – a scenario.

Each generation is cast to be different to the last. In this way the divide and rule strategy create divisions vertically to complement the horizontal division between those within each generation.

When I recall the **memorable** events of my Life so far, there is always a common factor – **emotion**. Grief, Joy, Relief, Agony, Love. The emotion of the moments differs but it is the **intensity** that sears them into my conscious memory.

It is (in part) only by **feeling** the emotion that you can re-call it or replicate it. An immortal soul does not understand many of the emotions we learn e.g. Grief. As an immortal being you can never experience death / loss, nor can you appreciate how unity (family) is stronger than separation.

The irony that our Higher Selves do not know who they are, where they came from, or why they are here (wherever here is) is the ultimate paradox but still answerable.

How can all paradoxes be resolved? It's a Game.

"From a little spark may burst a mighty flame"

We are all sharing a strange and peculiar experience called Life. For most people it just is. For some it is more than just existing. It is a puzzle, which frustrates and delights in equal measure. Most of us give up trying to puzzle it out and just get on with it. I should know as that was me for 56 years!

My story so far, is just that – a story. It will be forgotten the same as everybody else's, washed away by time. I'm a little over 2 years on my Awakening path and have been lucky, blessed, and protected to have the time and space to do so.

Like all things, it has become easier over time. In the beginning all I really wanted was reassurance that I wasn't going completely insane. If you've been feeling the same, let these words reassure you that you're **not** alone.

After that, I have primarily been interested in developing one thing – **knowledge**. It is a bottomless well, but it is also what really separates us. Knowledge like everything has a polarity with Knowing at one end and Ignorance at the other. I'm compelled to Know.

As many learning has progressed, so has my identity. I no longer solely identify as being Human. I know I am some sort of Spiritual awareness experiencing a material existence.

My Ego isn't dead, but most of it has been filed away along with all the other earlier iterations. I've found what was buried at the bottom of the pile and when I did, I **knew** it was me all along.

When I re-look at our species from outside the box, I see billions of mini dramas playing out to the music of Demons. I've probably seen worse, but this Game is fiendishly complex, and (almost) impossible to comprehend. I hope we **all** wake up.

There's a lot I enjoy about being Human. Helping people feels a good thing to do, so I'll keep doing that. Being with family regularly (not all the time lol) is always a good experience. Watching **their** stories unfold is interesting and pleasing. I try not to interfere in their Lives, but just be there when needed.

It took a while for the anger I felt over the deceptive nature of our existence to subside. The hidden control structure is beyond Machiavellian, and it was only by looking beyond it for deeper truth's that I was able to dampen the fire within.

I surrendered to the process the moment I knew that to do otherwise was futile. I have never been in control of anything in my Life. My Higher Self has already planned it out. I'm in this because **I wanted to**, I just don't remember.

It feels like it's been a hard path to follow, but I've no regrets as I didn't really have any choice **and** I'm in a better place than I was. It's been hard to **allow** things to happen, but free-will really is an illusion.

I tried very hard to take control of my Awakening. As time progressed, I felt a sense of impatience like that of a spoilt child. I wanted to **know**, and I wanted to know **Now!**

My Awakening didn't respond to that. At least not for me. It took time for the concepts to be accepted by my conscious mind. I was taken back to certain topics until they sunk in, only then could I go further, deeper.

The more resigned I became to allowing things to unfold as they will and letting go of all expectations, I found myself living in the **now**.

Thankfully I have no knowing of exactly what will unfold next, so my feelings of surprise, joy, and grief, are not contrived. These are the moments that linger longest and are just so - emotional.

As a teenager and young man, I read quite a lot of Science Fiction and Fantasy: C.S. Lewis, Azimov, A.E. Van Vogt, Heinlein, Tolkien, Arthur C. Clarke etc. Of all of them, it's Childhood's End, by the latter that keeps coming to mind.

It describes the next stage of an imagined Human evolution, featuring extra-terrestrials, and unfolds over many decades. Ultimately the novel concludes with the last generation of Homo Sapiens watching their enhanced children leave for the stars.

Whether or not it's a Happy Ending depends on the readers point of view.

It could be that Humanity is indeed approaching the next evolutionary stage as a species. The portents are writ large for those with eyes to see. The quest to augment Humans with technology and defy mortality is the stuff of tragedy.

And that appears to be exactly the direction we are being herded in. It won't end well, **but** from its end there will be a new beginning, and that's more than enough reason to observe how events unfold.

Right now, it is an epic tale of how Humanity is enslaved by monsters, who wish to defy God by using technology to re-write the divine blueprint of life and live forever. The irony being that they are **already** immortal as spiritual beings, but just want to stick the finger up to God.

Humanity is best characterised as a collective of fully grown children who accept everything, they are told by anyone or anything who they accept as an Authority. Deliberately dumbed down and subjected to constant mental stress to generate emotional energy for something else to consume.

The existential path for (99.9%) is a life of servitude. We are born into it. We arrive with nothing and must **earn** our right to exist, either by work, or by allegiance to the system, or both. Freedom of thought is closely managed, so most will never be consciously aware of their imprisonment. It's very **very** clever.

However! Everything changes all the time. I still exist within this system, but I have no allegiance to it. If it collapses, it will not be by my hand. I don't wish to play any part in its destruction, but I'll be watching with interest to see what part I can play (if any) in its re-birth.

I've read that Earth is the toughest school in the Universe and I have no reason to doubt it. **Every** Human is a hero. I don't know if I've penetrated through all the veils or if I'll ever transcend this Game, but I **will** continue to play.

We exist within an enclosed system, even our bodies are made up of elements derived from the Planet. When the body dies, its elements are returned, however while **my** Life force animates it, **I** have recognised that **I** own my Human body. It is **mine**. It is Sovereign and defers to none but has no authority beyond that.

Over time I have **chosen** to feel serene unless I **want** to feel differently. Most of the time I don't feel anything at all, which may sound terrible, but I can assure you it's **not**. My suffering is much **less** now than it was before Awakening.

I still experience aches and pains, but I inhabit a mortal body and its part of being Human, so I accept them without complaint (usually but not after a fencing job!). Almost as soon as I began my Awakening, I wanted to stop being a Handyman – it seemed so unimportant by comparison.

I was wrong again. It has helped me more than I can write down here, but at the beginning of 2023 I decided to put it up for sale. I'm getting too old for its physical demands, and everything changes eventually.

Since my 'shaking episode' the only physical thing I've noticed is that my appetite for food is much less than before. I haven't lost any weight although sometimes I have difficulty eating (anything) at all. It's a bit weird and hard to describe, but I'm sure it'll pass.

I've read that Awakening triggers changes within the individuals DNA, which can cause physical symptoms such as I've experienced. Everyone's experience is unique to them, and I'm not really worried about mine.

I've also read in several places that the highest destination on the Spiritual journey for incarnated Humans is that of the Christ consciousness, where upon the final destruction of the false ego, the individual concerned is endowed with the ultimate compassion of God.

Much as I would **like** to believe it, **I don't**. Where are these individuals? Why haven't they waved a wand and created Heaven on Earth long ago, unless it's just another deception, or if they **have** arisen, they have **not** intervened.

Having distanced myself from the Hermetic Principles I have nevertheless applied them to this goal only to find a paradox. Ultimate compassion, at its extreme, meets its opposing polarity - Ultimate indifference or un-compassion. It appears the creator has a twisted sense of humour.

It would be a fitting paradox that the only way to transcend the Game is to be totally indifferent toward it. For now, it seems a good a strategy as any. As such, I no longer care what might or might not happen **outside** of my lived experience, as in, I really don't give a shit.

Is it not true that the most compassionate thing anyone can do is to not interfere? Allowing everything and everyone just to be, **whatever it is they want to be**, is **both** compassionate and indifferent. I have found no discernible difference.

I don't want to waste any more of my emotional energy – positive or negative on something that is manifestly false i.e. The system. It is unworthy of it. I will simply abide by the Golden Rule:

Do unto others how you would have them do unto you. It is in the Spirit of this that I have written this book. If it helps someone else on their journey it will have been worth writing it.

As time progresses, I find myself observing more than doing and finding less and less to say. In one of Q's posts, it says 'the deeper you go the more unrealistic it becomes'. So perhaps I'm close to something that's mostly true. Lol.

I understand now why the fictional caricatures of humanity like the Munchkins in the Wizard of Oz or the Lilliputians in Gulliver's travels were created. When looked at objectively, Humanity is a caricature in its own right, so dysfunctional that it almost defies logic.

I don't have any beliefs anymore. The things I have written here form the basis of an overarching hypothesis from where I currently observe. Should my observations change, so will my hypothesis.

I'm an undergraduate student in the University of Life writing up his dissertation, ready to present it to my Tutor, except my Tutor isn't **here**. Perhaps they've already read it. Time is a very interesting phenomenon.

I am very grateful to be able to have a hot shower every day and live a life that does little or no harm. I do not crave special abilities or the power to work miracles. What would I do with them anyway? The World is already perfectly imperfect.

I have found what I spent my Life unconsciously looking for......... **Me**.

If you made it to here, thank **you** for your attention. Now do your own research and pay attention!

We are here to Learn, and nothing really matters. It's a Game.

An Outside the Box solution (there are more than one):

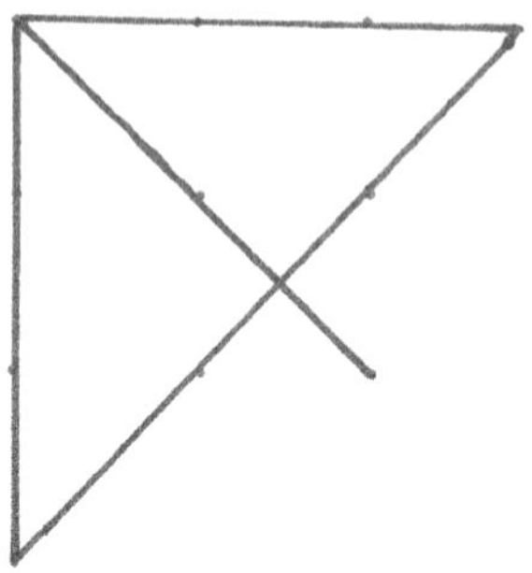

About the Author

Robert Butterwick lives in the village of Eye in Cambridgeshire with his wife Lesley and their two rescue Dogs – Loki, a Spanish Spaniel and Bruno (but we don't talk about him).

All feedback and comments are welcome, unless you're a Troll, in which case your nonsense will be laughed at.

He can be contacted via info@oddjobbob.co.uk

Printed in Great Britain
by Amazon

23763263R00089